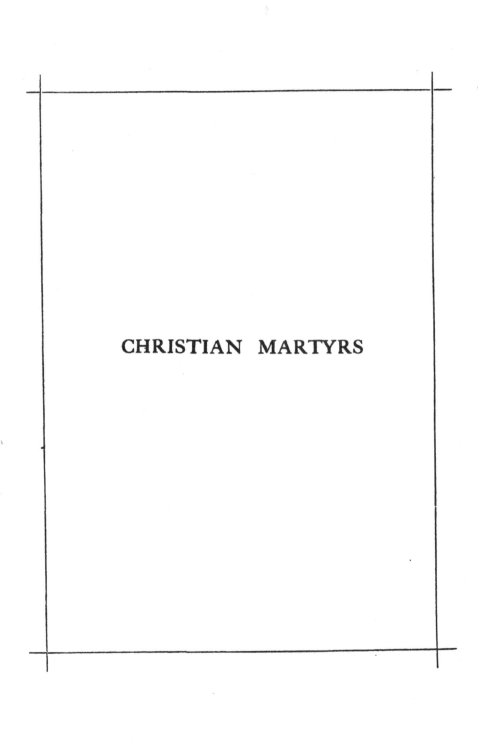

CHRISTIAN MARTYRS

Tortures and Torments

OF THE

Christian Martyrs

FROM THE "DE SS. MARTYRUM CRUCIATIBUS"
OF THE REV. FATHER GALLONIO

NOW FOR THE FIRST TIME TRANSLATED AND ADAPTED

By A. R. ALLINSON, M.A. Oxon.

"Others had Trial of cruel Mockings and Scourgings, yea, moreover, of Bonds and Imprisonment: they were Stoned, they were Sawn asunder, they were Tempted, they were Slain with the Sword: they went about in Sheepskins, in Goatskins; being Destitute, Afflicted, Evil Entreated."—*St. Paul, Hebrews* xi. 36, 37.

*ILLUSTRATED WITH THE FORTY-SIX ORIGINAL PLATES
AND PUBLISHER'S NOTE CONCERNING THE ORIGIN AND SCOPE OF THE BOOK.*

London and Paris
LIMITED EDITION
PRINTED FOR THE SUBSCRIBERS
1903

PUBLISHER'S NOTE

RESPECTING THE ORIGIN AND SCOPE OF
THE PRESENT BOOK

ONE often hears that certain Tortures were inflicted on the first Christians, but, beyond a few vague hints scattered here and there, it is impossible for unlettered folk to imagine the nature of the sufferings they were made to endure.

A perusal of the following pages will prove sufficiently edifying.

Probably no more awful lesson of Man's inhumanity to man, concentrated into so short a space, can be found throughout the annals of literature.

We deem a set preface hardly necessary to present this work to the Christian public. With an eloquence —terrible in its sheer realism—it speaks for itself, and must surely find favour in the eyes of earnest Catholic and Protestant alike.

Before the grim shadow of Pain and Death mere theological differences cease to exist.

The devout man, fretting at the little annoyances he may nowadays be subject to, will here see what nameless cruelties his spiritual forefathers bore some two thousand years ago, rather than, like Peter, "deny their Lord that bought them."

An English Doctor of Divinity, once well known in Paris, with whom I was conversing on this subject, said to me, in reply to an observation I had made on the barbarities done in the name of Religion :—

"But, my dear sir, you do not seem to realise that it must be far more painful for the people who torture heretics than it is for heretics to undergo the torture itself."

I confess that I have neither the ability nor the inclination to philosophise on such a point. The idea of studied cruelty, whether to man, woman, or child, causes me pain. When we ponder on the abominations wrought on high-souled women and girls, whose tender bodies were torn to pieces, whilst a word of recantation would have saved them—the word they resolutely refused to utter—when we think of the brave, noble-minded men who sang hymns of joy while they were being done to death, our amazement is divided between the marvellous heroism of the sufferers and the cold-blooded callousness of the man-shaped fiends who wrought them such wrong.

Verily these latter little foresaw how "the blood of the Martyrs would prove to be the seed of the Church."

At first sight, the subject of this book may appear to some minds repellent and unreal ; but on closer examination we find ourselves wondering—nay, stricken with admiration and astonishment—at the moral grandeur of the men and women who held with such fierce grip and tenacity "the Faith once delivered to the Saints."

If we were, for a moment, tempted to regard these records rather in the light of the nightmare ravings of a diseased brain, or the crazy imaginings of some narcotised wretch of over-weird humour, we should be quickly undeceived.

For every page bristles with documentary evidence attesting the authenticity of the cases adduced.

Father Gallonio has left no room for doubt!

It is sometimes said that torturing quite as barbarous would take place again to-day if it were possible.

For myself, I honestly and absolutely disbelieve in the possibility of this.

Men have changed: the old tigerish instinct has been conjured and subdued. Men are more humane, and the sight of blood, the thought of pain and cruelty, is abhorrent to all who live in the great centres of Christian civilisation.

From particular and isolated cases of cruelty we have no right to make general deductions. Systematic torturing to-day on any extensive scale, such as recorded in this work, could not stand for a minute before the fierce and universal cry of indignation which would break forth from people of all sorts and conditions.

Lecky says finely :—

"Torture was abolished because in the progress of civilisation the sympathies of man became more expansive, their perceptions of the sufferings of others more acute, their judgments more indulgent, their actions more gentle. . . . The movement that destroyed torture was much less an intellectual than an emotional movement. It represented much less a discovery of the reason than an increased intensity of sympathy."

Now a word as to the origin of the book. This most curious work, which may be roughly characterised as a sort of Catholic and Continental *Foxe's Book of Martyrs*, and which, like the latter collection of horrors, enjoyed an enormous vogue in the Seventeenth and the earlier part of the Eighteenth Centuries, appeared originally at Rome in 1591.

It was compiled by a learned Ecclesiastic of that city, a member of the Italian branch of the Oratorian Fathers, and author of several other books of a similar edifying nature—*History of the Roman Virgins* (4to, 1591); *Lives of Certain Martyrs* (4to, 1597); as well as of a *Life of St. Philip Neri* (4to, 1600). *The Christian Martyrs* was published in the first instance in Italian, *Trattato degli instrumenti di martirio e delle varie maniere di martirizare, Rome, 1591*, a quarto adorned with a series of fine copper-plates from the designs of Giovanni de Guerra of Modena, painter to Pope Sixtus V., engraved by Antonio Tempesta of Florence, representing all kinds of instruments of torture, and their various modes of application to the unhappy victims of persecution. Subsequently the Author translated his book into Latin, dedicating the version to Pope Clement VIII. It was issued under its new form at Rome in a quarto edition, 1594; and again at Paris, 4to, 1659, with the original plates reproduced. A 12mo edition was printed at Antwerp in 1660, followed by numerous other issues in the same *format* intended for popular use, manifestly "made to sell," and giving reduced and very inferior copies of Tempesta's plates, generally without any acknowledgment of their source.

These frequent editions bear witness to the great popularity of the little book, which outvied that of its English counterpart as much as the *De Cruciatibus* surpasses *The Book of Martyrs* both in gruesomeness and completeness.

Father Gallonio's work was intended for the edification of the Faithful, and was issued with the full authority and approbation of the Church.

But those conversant with the secrets of man's heart may be permitted to suspect a graver reason for its general acceptance than even the sanction of the Papal powers.

Deep down in our poor human nature lurks the love of blood, a remnant of the primeval beast happily slinking away before the dawn of the better times.

It is our deliberate conviction, therefore, that the prodigious vogue it enjoyed throughout Europe for so many years was largely, if not chiefly, due to the same morbid love of horrors that carried the Roman populace to the Coliseum, drew the London mob to Newgate and Tyburn, and the Parisians in their thousands to the Place de Grève to watch Damiens and Ravaillac done to death; and a few years ago (1892) attracted fashionable crowds to the horrible (but most interesting) Exhibition of Instruments of Torture, collected by the late Duke of Buckingham and Chandos, and thrown open by him to the London public.

Not the least remarkable thing about the *De Cruciatibus* is its profoundly systematic character, the careful classification and minute division and sub-division of tortures and instruments of torture, each duly ranged under its proper heading and category, the whole constituting, as it were, for all time, a complete and comprehensive Text-book of Torture.

We may recall a passage in Renan's Preface to his famous *L'Abbesse de Jouarre*, which throws a startling, and not very edifying, light on the circumstances attending, or rather immediately preceding, the moment of Martyrdom in many instances.

"There is one thing above all else," he writes, "bound to assume, in its final hour, a character of absolute and utter sincerity, and that is Love. I often picture to myself, supposing mankind should acquire the certainty that the world was to come to an end in two or three days, how Love would burst forth on all hands in a sort of uncontrollable phrenzy. . . . . This is precisely what happened to the Martyrs of the early Christian Church. The last night they spent together in prison gave occasion to scenes that Moralists could not but disapprove. These unions under the shadow of death were the natural consequences of the tragic situation, and the condition of exalted happiness which affects men and women brought into each other's company to die together for one and the same noble cause. In such a case, the body, so soon to be tortured, is as good as annihilated already. The spirit only is left dominant; the great leveller, Death, has destroyed all mundane scruples; the soul is verily and indeed by anticipation in the Kingdom of God."

Needless to say, not a word of this appears in the good Gallonio. All is for edification; and Martyrs,

Confessors, Virgins, one and all confront the diabolically cruel and blood-curdling torments our Author describes in such minute detail in the most pious frame of mind and with the most imperturbable serenity.

The present English version is the first that has appeared, and follows the original Italian and Latin texts very closely. The only liberties the Translator has taken with his Author are two. First, the omission of the long lists of perfectly obscure and entirely unknown Saints whom Gallonio scrupulously records as having perished under such-and-such a form of martyrdom. This meticulous parade of names, though doubtless gratifying to their owners, always supposing the *De Cruciatibus* to be studied in Paradise, could only be a weariness of the flesh to the modern reader.

For a similar reason the pious prayers and edifying exhortations with which the good Father liberally decorates his pages, though doubtless giving a *local colour* agreeable to some minds, have been somewhat cut down in number and prolixity. On the other hand, the fine original plates of the quarto edition have been reproduced with the utmost fidelity, being indeed absolutely indispensable to the complete understanding of the text.

Father Gallonio's work was well worthy of resuscitation.

It appeals with equal strength of interest to many different classes of readers.

In these pages, the earnest Christian, to whatever sect or branch of the Universal Church he belong, will

Publisher's Note

learn how perfectly trifling are the inconveniences he is called upon to face in these times when compared with the unutterable cruelties the first followers of the Great Master suffered as the price of bearing His name.

The student of civilisation will rejoice at the progress made since these things were possible; for do they not attest that man has risen and is rising still to a higher moral plane?

Weary and long has been the march; knee-deep in fields of gore the human caravan has often had to wade. Here it has had to break through forests of error, there to traverse illimitable desert tracks of pain, and the hearts of the pilgrims have often been heavy with woe. In the night's darkness they have cried to their God, and no God hath answered; or is it that "their ears were holden so that they should not hear"?

We see them, these scarred-faced hosts, wending their way across the centuries of desolation and unending struggle; their visage is pain-torn, their brows perplexed. But, all unconsciously, they have been coming towards the Light. They are now at the foot of the mountain they shall climb; the mists are slowly lifting. Shall they not one day attain the summit? May there not be some truth after all in the words of promise that "God shall wipe away all tears from their eyes"?

THOSE WHO CANNOT BELIEVE MAY WORK ON AND HOPE.   C. C.

PARIS, 1st January, 1903.

CONTENTS

Contents

ILLUSTRATIONS

Illustrations

TORTURES AND TORMENTS

OF THE

CHRISTIAN MARTYRS

CHAPTER I

Of the Cross, of Stakes, and other Means whereby the bodies of Christians remaining steadfast in their Confession of Christ were suspended

SEEING we do propose in this book to treat of the divers instruments of Martyrdom and of the countless modes wherein the most glorious and unconquered soldiers of our Lord Jesus Christ underwent death with a brave heart for His honour, we have judged it proper to begin our task with the blessed and holy Cross. For this it was whereon the Saviour of the World, bursting the bonds of death, did vanquish that cunning serpent, the Devil, and by His sufferings earned for His servants so great fortitude as that they were ready in gladness of spirit to endure the most arduous hardships of every sort,

1

even, if need were, to the shedding of their blood and the most cruel lopping off of all their limbs. Forasmuch, therefore, as these professors and preachers of the sacred and divine Law won from the Cross that strength they did display in tortures and torments, it hath seemed to us meet and becoming to put the Cross first in this our book. But whereas stakes set up in the ground were included by the Ancients under the common name of cross, we must accordingly treat of these likewise in the same chapter, as well as of divers other modes wherein the bodies of the Blessed Martyrs were suspended as punishment for defending of the Faith of Christ ; for, indeed, whether nailed to the cross or bound to wooden poles, they may equally be said in a sense to have hung suspended.

But to return to the Cross, we may say that not only were the Jews accustomed to nail condemned criminals to the cross, but the Gentiles likewise. And this is expressly stated by sundry of their own authors—in the first place by Cicero in several places (especially in the *Philippics* and *De Finibus*), also by Valerius Maximus, by Livy, Curtius, Suetonius (*Galba*), and Seneca (*De Consolatione*). This last passage shows that crosses were of more than one kind, as is plain from the words hereunder quoted : "From this I gather that crosses were not all of one kind, but differently made by different people. Some there are who hang the criminal head downwards, while others drive a stake through his entrails, and others again stretched out his arms on a forked gallows," etc. Now as for what he says here, "others drive a stake through his entrails," what sort of cross this was, the same Seneca doth elsewhere explain; for he calls this kind of cross, in his indictment of the luxurious Mecænas, a sharp-pointed cross. From which anyone may readily understand that, while one form of cross was like those we commonly designate by the word *cross*, another resembled the sharp stakes which at the present day the Turks employ for executing criminals, driving them through the victims' middle up to the head. Read also Procopius, *Vandal War.*

On the first kind of Cross (as Seneca states in the above passage, and numerous *Acts* of the Saints bear witness) some were fixed with their heads toward the ground, others with them raised to heaven. In both these ways were the Christian martyrs crucified by the worshippers of idols. Amongst others which won the crown of martyrdom by crucifixion head downwards was the chief of the Apostles himself, St. Peter, concerning whom Origen writes thus: "When Peter was come to the outskirts of Rome, with head placed downwards (for so he desired himself to suffer), he was nailed to the Cross."

St. Augustine again writes: "So both (Peter and Paul) hasten to attain to the palm of martyrdom, and win the crown thereof." And a little lower down: "Peter for Christ's sake is suspended on the tree head downward; Paul slain with the sword. The Apostle went with his own feet to meet Christ, and looking upward with his eyes to heaven, sent forth his blessed spirit to the heavens above." To the same purport (to pass over other Fathers) St. Chrysostom (*Homily on the Chief of the*

Apostles) : "Rejoice, Peter, to whom hath been vouchsafed to enjoy Christ on the tree, and who wast fain to be crucified as thy Master was, yet not with form upright like Christ the Lord, but with head turned to the ground, as one journeying from earth to heaven. Blessed the nails which did pierce those holy limbs." Thus Chrysostom. To this most holy Apostle of Christ may be further added St. Calliopus, which died the same death for guarding the Christian Faith, and bravely and signally did triumph over the World and the Devil. So much, then, for Martyrs crucified with feet upward towards the sky.

But with feet pointing to the ground (to continue our theme) there suffered many clarion-voiced champions of the Christian Law,—for instance, St. Philip and St. Andrew, Apostles ; Nestor, a Bishop ; Timon, a Deacon, and others. Beside these, moreover, the *Roman Martyrology* tells of ten thousand Martyrs so crucified, and in special a certain Simeon, a Bishop, who at the date of his Martyrdom was in the one hundred and twentieth year of his age. Concerning the first-named, that is, the ten thousand that were lifted up on the Cross (22 June), we read : "On Mount Ararat the passion of ten thousand blessed Martyrs which were crucified." Concerning St. Simeon (20 April): "At Jerusalem anniversary of the Blessed Simeon, Bishop and Martyr, which is said to have been son of Cleophas and a kinsman of the Saviour according to the flesh. Ordained Bishop of Jerusalem next after James, brother of Our Lord, after suffering in the persecution of Trajan many tortures, he died a Martyr, all present and the very

FIG. I.

A. Martyrs suspended by one foot.
B. Suspended by both feet.
C. Raised on the cross, head uppermost.
D. Nailed to the cross, head downwards. ‡

E. Hung up by both arms, heavy weights being attached to the feet.
F. Christian women suspended by the hair.
G. Martyrs hung up by one arm only, ponderous stones being fastened to their feet.

4a

To face p. 4

Judge himself marvelling how an old man of an hundred and twenty years should have endured the punishment of the Cross bravely and unflinchingly." The same Bishop Simeon is commemorated likewise by Eusebius (*Ecclesiastical History*).

MODE EMPLOYED BY THE HEATHEN FOR CRUCIFYING THE CHRISTIANS.

In the first place, the ministers of cruelty would make ready (as sundry passages from the *Acts of the Saints* above referred to, and particularly those of St. Pionius, do manifest) mallet, iron nails, and a cross made of wood, which they then set on the ground, sometimes attaching ropes thereto, for fastening to the hands and feet of such as were to be crucified. Then laying the holy Martyrs, or it may be others of their own vain religion which had been condemned for some crime, on the wood, after stripping them of their clothes, they hung them by means of four (such would seem most probably to have been the number) nails thereon. This done, they raised the cross along with the victims fixed to the same, and setting it up in a hole dug out for the purpose, left them to the bitter agony of a lingering death,—hanging there till they rotted away, as Valerius Maximus in several passages clearly implies. From this we may gather that the Jews differed from the Gentiles with regard to removing the bodies of those crucified from the cross. The latter, as we have just noted, left them to hang on the gibbet till they rotted ; but the Jews did otherwise, for in accord with the Law as declared in *Deuteronomy*, ch. xxi., they were used to take them down the same day and bury them in a convenient place.

Secondly, of the other sort of Cross, which we did show at the beginning of the chapter, on Seneca's authority, to have been a sharp stake, we shall say little in the present work, forasmuch as hitherto we have been unable to find in the histories of the ancient Martyrs any record of such a punishment being inflicted, unless indeed we choose to include under this head the torture inflicted on certain most glorious athletes of Christ by having pointed sticks driven through their inwards. But of this, an if God favour us, we shall treat in the last chapter of our book. Another partly similar punishment is described by Theodoret (*Ecclesiastical History*) in the following words : "But when he beholds him (St. Benjamin) making mock of this torture, he commands yet another reed to be pushed this time into his genital member, the which reed being drawn out and pushed in again, did cause him inexpressible torments. Afterward the savage tyrant orders a stout rod, thick and extremely rough by reason of branches that stuck out all over it, to be inserted up his fundament." So far Theodoret. It is a fact, moreover, that the Turks impaled on stakes Hadrian of the Order of St. Dominic and twenty-six others, his companions ; and the like punishment is spoke of by Procopius (*Vandal War*). But of this enough.

OF STAKES.

Stakes were largely employed and in manifold ways by the heathen Devil-worshippers for the tormenting of Christians. Fastening the blessed Martyrs thereto, after stripping their bodies as near naked as might be, either by means of iron nails or with ropes, they would then tear their flesh mercilessly with claws of iron or hooks or currycombs, transfix them with arrows, beat them with cudgels, scourges, and the like, expose them to the bites of wild beasts, pull out their teeth, cut out their tongues, in the case of women amputate the bosoms, in a word torture them in every horrid fashion possible, after first attaching them to stakes or poles set in the ground.

This is confirmed by numberless *Acts* of the Holy Martyrs, as those of Gregory Thaumaturgus, Polycarp, Gaiana, and Febronia, Virgins, and a well-nigh countless host of others of either sex. The same is shown likewise by Classical authors, amongst the rest by Cicero (*Philippics*), Valerius Maximus, Suetonius (*Claudius*), etc.

It should be noted here that the Martyrs which were nailed to stakes with iron nails and so tortured, were sometimes also bound with ropes, it may be for their yet greater torment.

OF PILLARS AND TREES, EMPLOYED FOR THE SAME, OR THE LIKE, PURPOSE.

Albeit the Worshippers of Devils were most often used to punish those condemned to death after binding them to stakes or crosses, yet it is found sometimes recorded of our Martyrs how that they were tied up to pillars or trees, or nailed to the same with nails, at the command of their tormentors, and so tortured.

Of pillars so used the *Acts* of sundry Martyrs as well as Eusebius bear witness. Then, lastly, there is the famous Pillar religiously preserved in the Basilica of St. Sebastian outside the Walls, which is believed in accord with ancient Christian tradition to be the very same whereto the said Blessed Martyr was bound and shot to death with arrows for confessing his faith in Christ.

Similarly of trees so employed the *Acts* of divers Martyrs, such as those of St. Zoé and of St. Paphnutius, do bear record.

OF DIVERS MODES OF SUSPENDING FROM THE CROSS, ETC.

Having sufficiently treated of the Cross itself and of Stakes used for crucifixion, it now remains in this latter part of the chapter to inquire into the modes of suspending from the same; that is to say in what ways the Blessed Martyrs and champions of the Holy Gospel were hung therefrom by the Heathen. For both various and horribly cruel are the methods of hanging, the which we find them suffering at the caprice of their tormentors. Of some we read how they were suspended by one foot only, others by both feet, or else (as Nicephorus describes in his *History*) by one foot drawn up to the level of the head, a slow fire being kindled underneath in such wise as to suffocate them with the smoke coming from

FIG. II.

A. Martyr suspended by both feet, and a great stone fastened to his neck.
B. Sometimes the Blessed Martyrs, after being smeared with honey, were bound to stakes fixed in the ground, and so exposed to the rays of the sun, to be tortured by the stings of flies and bees.
C. Martyr suspended by one foot; one leg is bent at the knee, which is constricted by means of an iron ring, the other being weighted with a heavy mass of iron.

To face p. 8

the burning fuel. Yet others were suspended by the arms, both or only one, or else by the tips of the thumbs, heavy and unconscionable weights being attached at the same time to the feet. Of others again we find it recorded that they were suspended hanging from a high wall, stones being fastened to neck and feet, or ropes bound to their bodies, their shoulders loaded with great lumps of salt, and for their greater torment wooden gags being put in their mouth. It is stated further of certain others, how that they were anointed with honey, and so attached to upright stakes under a blazing sun, to be tortured by the stings of flies and bees. Others are said to have been suspended from iron hooks, or from a noose, till they were dead, being hanged in fact in the same way as robbers and murderers are put to death in our own days. Last of all, they were tied up to pillars, their faces turned toward each other, with the feet not reaching the ground, or else hung up by the hair, as was often done to women contending for the Faith of Christ.

Of all these several modes the *Acts* of the Blessed Martyrs make frequent mention—of the first in especial the *Acts* of St. Gregory, Bishop of Armenia.

Christian women, likewise, were often hung up by one foot the whole day long (as Eusebius, *Ecclesiastical History*, doth bear witness), in such a way that not even their privy parts were covered, for to show the greatest possible scorn of Christ's holy Religion.

However, as concerns the modes wherein the Martyrs were tortured by suspension, these were many and divers.

Sometimes they were simply hung up by one foot, while at others smoke from damp and evil-smelling fuel, such as the dung of animals, was added to increase the agony, and to crown all, a dozen executioners thrashing the victim at the same time with rods.   In other instances they were suspended by one foot, the leg being bent at the knee and an iron band fixed round that joint, and then an iron weight fastened to the other foot in such a way that the unhappy victims were miserably strained asunder.   Thus in the *Acts* of St. Samona we find it thus written : " But the Magistrate at once orders Samona to have one leg bent at the knee and an iron band put around the joint.   This done, he hangs him head down by the foot of the bent leg, at the same time dragging the other downwards by means of an iron weight."

Of Martyrs which suffered by the first of these modes of torment, we read amongst others the names of those most noble soldiers of Christ mentioned a little above, St. Gregory of Armenia and St. Samona.

As to the second mode, whereby the victims were hung up by both feet, sundry *Acts* of the Saints speak of this,—for example, those of St. Venantius, of the holy Virgins Euphemia and her sisters, of Bishop Acepsima and his companions.   Also the Cappadocian Martyrs, a great host commemorated in the *Roman Martyrology*, under May 23, where it is thus written : "In Cappadocia, commemoration of the Blessed Martyrs which in the persecution of Maximianus were slain and their limbs broken ; likewise of those which at the same date in Mesopotamia were hung aloft by the feet head down, suffocated with smoke, and consumed over a slow fire, and so fulfilled their Martyrdom."

But verily it was not in one way only, but in many and divers, that the Martyrs were suspended by these Servants of the Devil (as may be gathered from the *Acts* above quoted) and tormented. For sometimes they were suffocated with smoke; sometimes their heads pounded with hammers by their executioners; sometimes great stones fastened round their necks; sometimes again cruelly burned with blazing torches.

In the first of these ways many Christians are known to have suffered in the region of Mesopotamia; in the second, Euphemia, Thecla, Erasma, and Dorothea, most noble Virgins and Martyrs of Christ; in the third, Saints Theopompus, Mercurius and the already mentioned Venantius.

OF THE THIRD MODE OF SUSPENDING, THAT IS, OF MARTYRS HUNG UP BY ONE ARM.

This third mode of suspending, to wit, as we say, hanging up by one arm, is mentioned in very many *Acts* of the Blessed Martyrs, among which we may reckon those of St. Samona just cited, as also those of St. Antonia, that most noble-hearted martyr, concerning whom it is thus found recorded in the *Roman Martyrology*, under May 4: "At Nicomedia, the anniversary of St. Antonia, Martyr, who, after being savagely racked and tortured with divers torments, suspended three days by one arm, and kept imprisoned two years in a dungeon, was finally burned at the stake by the Governor Priscillianus, confessing the Lord Jesus." Thus the *Roman Martyrology*.

In the first place we should notice that sometimes the executioners of Martyrs suspended in this way were accustomed, to the end that all the several joints of their bodies might be drawn asunder, to fasten stones of great weight to their feet. Of this fact noble and undoubted testimony is given us by the *Histories* of divers Saints, especially that of St. Samona already quoted in another connection in the present chapter.

OF WEIGHTS, WHEREWITH THE ATHLETES OF OUR LORD JESUS CHRIST WERE TORTURED.

We read again and again in the *Histories* of the Martyrs how, after being suspended aloft, they were, among other torments, loaded with weights, of which some were of lead or iron (as we shall describe elsewhere), others again of stone. Of the latter we have evidence in sundry such, that are preserved to this day here in Rome in the Churches of the Holy Apostles, as also in those of St. Apollinaris and St. Anastasius not far from the City. They were stones of great weight, black in colour, round or oval in shape, having an iron ring imbedded in the stone, through which a rope for binding and hanging could be passed and so attached to the feet or hands of those suspended.

Another thing we would not have the reader ignorant of, that certain authorities have maintained the opinion that

FIG. III.

A. Martyr suspended by his thumbs, heavy stones being attached to his feet.

B. Christians hung up, and a slow fire kindled underneath, so as to suffocate them with the smoke; the victims being scourged meantime with rods.

12a

the aforesaid stone balls, called by Josephus (*Maccabees*) *Orbicularia*, or Round Stones, were not designed specially for purposes of inflicting torture, but for weighing. This cannot possibly be so, as is proved in the notes appended to the *Roman Martyrology;* for stones of this kind always had (as Isidore and Alciatus, *On Weights*, state) the figure of the weight inscribed on them, which these evidently have not.

These weights were entirely different from those to which debtors were condemned in Law XII. of the "Twelve Tables," these latter being nothing more than fetters. Of them Aulus Gellius speaks, saying thus, "Bind him either with a thong, or else with fetters of not less than fifteen pounds' weight; or if a greater weight be desired, with heavier still."

OF THE FOURTH MODE OF SUSPENDING, THAT IS TO SAY HANGING BY BOTH ARMS.

This fourth method of suspending is mentioned in the *Acts* of Saints Procopius, Andochius, Thyrsus and Felix, and others their companions.

Here you must know, that the custom of the Heathen was on occasion, either to attach heavy weights to the feet of those suffering this mode of hanging, or else after twisting their arms behind their backs to haul them aloft and then let them go. Thus in the *Roman Martyrology*, under September 24th, we read of those blessed Confessors of Christ, St. Andochius and his Companions : "At Augustodunun (Autun), the anniversary of the Holy Martyrs Andochius, Priest, Thyrsus, Deacon, and Felix, who being sent by the Blessed Polycarp, Bishop of Smyrna, from the East to teach Gaul Christianity, were there most cruelly scourged, and suspended all day with hands tied behind their backs and thrown into the fire, but not consumed. Finally their necks are struck with heavy bars, and they thus win the crown of martyrdom."

OF THE FIFTH MODE OF SUSPENDING, TO WIT HANGING UP BY THE THUMBS.

This fifth method is to be found described in the *Acts* of Saints Jacob and Marianus, wherein the following narrative is written concerning Marianus, servant of Christ: " But Marianus he condemned to torture, because he confessed himself a reader only, as indeed he was. And what torments were these, how new and strange, how instinct with the poisoned ingenuity of the Devil, how cunningly contrived to break the spirit! Marianus was hung up to be tortured ; and what grace the Martyr showed even in the midst of his sufferings, the very torment and punishment but exalting his courage! Now the cord which kept him suspended was attached not to his hands but to the tips of his thumbs, in such wise that the slenderness of those parts should add to the agony endured in supporting the weight of the rest of the body. Moreover unconscionable weights were further attached to the feet, so that the whole framework of the body should hang suspended, torn asunder by distracting pains and agonising convulsions of the inwards." So far the *Acts*; whereby is plainly shown the truth of what we have stated concerning this fifth mode of punishment.

OF THE SIXTH MODE, TO WIT HANGING UP WITH WEIGHTS FASTENED ROUND THE NECK AND TO THE FEET.

As to this method the *History* of the most Blessed Martyr St. Severianus bears witness, where it is thus written: "Accordingly the Prefect, taking Severianus' silence for contempt, as indeed it was, contrived a yet more terrible punishment for him; and after removing him from the rack, has him taken to a wall. Then after attaching two enormous and very heavy stones, one to his neck, the other to his feet, and tying a rope round the Martyr's middle, he leaves him hanging in the air from the wall, that his members being dragged asunder by the weights, he may perish in this violent fashion." Thus the *Acts*; but enough said, and more than enough, of this sixth form of cruelty.

OF THE SEVENTH, NAMELY WHEN THE SUFFERERS' BODIES ARE SUSPENDED BY ROPES, THEIR SHOULDERS AT THE SAME TIME BEING LOADED WITH HEAVY LUMPS OF SALT AND THE LIKE.

This seventh kind is mentioned in the *Acts* of St. Gregory of Armenia, where we read thus: "When St. Gregory had ended dilating at length on these matters, Tyridates was filled with anger above all measure, and furiously stirred up against him. Accordingly the most noble hero was instantly bound.

Then after they had inserted a wooden gag into his mouth, parting the upper and lower jaws as widely as possible, they loaded his shoulders with lumps of salt, which is dug up in Armenia. Then binding his holy body with ropes, they suspended the Saint aloft, prolonging this bitter torment for seven whole days." So far the *Acts* of St. Gregory, which (if the truth must be told) make very clearly manifest to us the nature and enormity of this mode of suspension.

OF THE EIGHTH MODE, TO WIT SUSPENDING THE VICTIMS FROM UPRIGHT STAKES, AFTER SMEARING THEM WITH HONEY, SO THAT THEY SHOULD BE TORTURED BY THE BITES OF FLIES AND BEES.

This form of torture is spoke of in the *Histories* of St. Maurice and his companions, and of St. Mark of Arethusa.

Three modes are to be found recorded in the *Histories* of the Martyrs wherein Christians were exposed to the rays of the sun with this end in view. Sometimes they were merely bound to stakes, as was done with St. Maurice and his companions ; sometimes they were raised aloft in baskets made of rushes, as may be read of St. Mark of Arethusa, named a little above ; lastly (as St. Jerome bears witness in the *History* of Paul, the first Eremite), they were sometimes laid on the ground with hands tied behind their backs.

Cœlius Rhodiginus states that there existed among the Ancients a form of punishment known as "Cyphonismus," so named from the word *Cyphon* (κύφων), "from which also Cyphon is so called in Aristophanes' play of *Plutus*," writes

FIG. IV.

A. Martyr suspended by the feet, and his head at the same time pounded with hammers.

B. Martyr suspended by the hands, which are tied behind his back, heavy weights being fastened to his feet and round his neck.

16a

To face p. 16

Rhodiginus, "because it was a sort of fetter of wood or, as in the present day, of iron, commonly styled a pillory," to which the prisoner was fastened by way of ignominy and there detained, smeared with honey and exposed to the bites of the flies. "Hence it came about," adds the same author, "that this title of 'Cyphon' was given to scamps, and the punishment was called 'Cyphonismus.'" Then again a little below: "I note among certain people a regulation to the following effect—that any man who shall have insolently thrown contempt on the decrees of the law, shall be kept in fetters at the public place of execution for twenty days, naked and smeared over with honey and milk, to be food for bees and flies; and when these have done their work, he shall be dressed in women's clothes and cast headlong down a cliff."

Of somewhat the same kind was a mode of punishment the Persians employed for criminals condemned to death, which they themselves called *Scaphismus*. Plutarch (*Artaxerxes*) speaks of it in these terms: "Accordingly he ordered Mithridates to be put to death by the punishment of the boats (*scaphae*). The nature of this form of death and punishment is as follows: Two boats being built of the same size and shape, in the one they lay the man destined for the torture, and putting the other atop of him, join the two together in such a way that his hands and feet are left outside, while the whole of the rest of his body (except the head) is imprisoned. They supply the man with food, and by prodding his eyes with sharp points force him to eat even against his will. But on his eating, they pour by way of drink into his mouth a mixture of milk and honey, and smear his face with the same. Also turning about the boat they so arrange it that his eyes are always facing the sun, and his head and face are covered every day with a host of flies that settle upon them. Moreover as he does inside the closed boats those things which men are bound of necessity to do after eating and drinking, the resulting corruption and putrefaction give birth to swarms of worms of divers sorts, which penetrating inside his clothes, eat away his flesh. For when, after the man is dead, the upper boat is removed, his body is seen to be all gnawed away, and all about his inwards is found a multitude of these and the like insects, that grows denser every day. Subjected to this form of torture, Mithridates actually endured the agonizing existence to the seventeenth day, before he finally gave up the ghost." Thus Plutarch, whose account differs but little from that given by Zonaras (*Annals*) in the following terms: "The Persians outvie all other Barbarians in the horrid cruelty of their punishments, employing tortures that are peculiarly terrible and long-drawn, namely the 'boats' and sewing men up in raw hides. But what is meant by the 'boats,' I must now explain for the benefit of less well informed readers. Two boats are joined together one on top of the other, with holes cut in them in such a way that the victim's head, hands, and feet only are left outside. Within these boats the man to be punished is placed lying on his back, and the boats then nailed together with bolts. Next they pour a mixture of milk and honey into the wretched man's mouth, till he is filled to the point of nausea, smearing his face, feet, and arms with the same mixture, and so leave him exposed to the sun. This is repeated every day, the effect being that flies, wasps, and bees, attracted by the sweetness, settle on his face and all such parts of him as project outside the boats, and miserably torment and sting the wretched man. Moreover his belly, distended as it is with milk and honey, throws off liquid excrements, and these putrefying breed swarms of worms, intestinal and of all sorts. Thus the victim lying in the boats, his flesh rotting away in his own filth and devoured by worms, dies a lingering and horrible death. By this punishment Parysatis, mother of Artaxerxes and Cyrus, is said to have executed the man who boasted of having slain Cyrus when contending with his brother for the Kingship; he endured the torment fourteen days before he died. Such then is the nature of 'Scaphismus,' or the boat-torture."

Something different the fate of those which were sewn up in an ox-hide. In this case the head alone was left outside, all the rest of the body being stripped naked and sewn up inside the hide. So we read in the *Acts* of St. Chrysanthus: "Carrying him away from that place, they proceeded to flay a calf, and to wrap him up naked in the fresh hide, placing him so as to face the sun; nevertheless, albeit exposed all day long to the excessive heat of a blazing sun, he could feel no especial warmth. But still continuing of the same freshness as at first, the hide could in no wise hurt God's servant. So afterward they laid on him fetters and the like." From this it is plainly evident how that this punishment of the raw hide was different and distinct from that just described under the name "Scaphismus."

Similar forms of torture may be found in plenty described in Lucian's *Dialogue* entitled *Lucius, or the Ass,* wherein the following story is related : "We must discover," he then said, "some sort of death whereby this maiden may endure long-drawn and bitter torment. . . . So let us kill this ass, and afterwards cut open its belly and after removing the inwards, shut up the girl inside in such a way that only her head be left outside (this to prevent her being entirely suffocated), while the rest of her body be hid within the carcase. Then, when this hath been sewn up, let us expose them both to the vultures—a strange meal prepared in a new and strange fashion. Now just consider the nature of this torture, I beg you. To begin with, a living woman will be shut up inside a dead ass ; then by reason of the heat of the sun will she be roasted within its belly ; further, she will be tormented with mortal hunger, yet entirely unable to destroy herself. Yet other features of her agony, both from the stench of the dead body as it rots, and the swarm of writhing worms, I say nothing of. Lastly, the vultures that feed on the carcase will rend in pieces the living woman at the same time. All shouted assent to this monstrous proposal, and unanimously approved its being put in execution."

To the same effect Apuleius in his *Golden Ass,* who writes thus: "Let us decide to cut this ass's throat to-morrow, and when it hath been cleared of all the entrails, to sew the virgin naked into the middle of its belly, so that only the girl's face

Fig. V.

A. Martyr suspended by the hands, which are bound behind his back, and having the shoulders weighted with lumps of salt, a wooden gag being also forced into his mouth.
B. Martyr suspended by a hook.

To face p. 20

project, while all the rest of her be imprisoned within the animal, and this done, to expose the ass with its contents on some craggy height to the exhalations of the blazing sun."

OF THE NINTH AND TENTH MODES OF HANGING, TO WIT SUSPEND-
ING FROM A HOOK AND PUTTING TO DEATH WITH A NOOSE.

These two modes of Martyrdom be amply attested in divers *Acts* of the Blessed Martyrs—in the first place by those of St. Nicetus, as also of Saints Gorgonius and Dorotheus, whose deaths are likewise recorded by Eusebius in his *Ecclesiastical History*.

OF THE ELEVENTH MODE, TO WIT BINDING THE VICTIMS TO
PILLARS WITH FEET NOT TOUCHING THE GROUND.

This fashion is spoke of by Bishop Philæas, as quoted by Eusebius in his *Ecclesiastical History*, as follows : "Others again were bound facing each other, suspended from pillars with their feet not reaching the ground, in such a way that the greater the strain put upon the ropes and the tighter these were drawn, the more cruelly did the victims feel the agony caused by the dragging weight of their own bodies. Nor was it for a short while only, just while the Magistrate was putting them to cross-examination, and was at liberty to question them, but pretty well all day long they endured this kind of torment. Moreover when, as he went on from them to others, he left officers subordinate to his authority to watch carefully the first batch, if so be any of them should seem like being overmastered and yielding to the torture, giving orders that they be racked by means of the ropes without an instant's respite, and finally, when on the point of giving up the ghost, that they be let down again to the ground and dragged unmercifully to and fro."

The same writer saith in the same sense a little higher up, "Others were suspended from the portico or arch, attached by one arm, and did endure the stretching and straining of all their limbs and joints,—a bitter torment surpassing almost every other in severity. Others again were bound to pillars, their faces turned inward toward one another, with nothing for their feet to rest upon."

Now as to the fashion wherein the Martyrs were lashed to the pillars, we should understand there were fastened to the upper portions of these pillars either iron rings or, more likely still, sundry pulleys, over which ropes were led. By means of these ropes the Blessed Martyrs were then, with arms tied behind their backs and faces turned toward the pillars, all day long first hoisted up by the tormentors, and afterward let down again with a rush, yet in such wise that they never quite touched the ground, this being done that they might suffer the more agonising pain. Finally, when they were on the point of yielding up the ghost, the executioners, at a sign from the Judge, would lower them to the earth again and drag them cruelly hither and thither.

OF THE LAST MODE, TO WIT OF CHRISTIAN WOMEN HUNG UP BY THE HAIR.

Of this fashion of torture witness is to be found in very many *Histories* of the Holy Martyrs; in the first place in the account of the passion of St. Eulampia, St. Juliana, virgin and martyr, as also of Saints Theonilla, Euphemia, and lastly, St. Symphorosa.

So much we have deemed it well to say concerning the divers modes of suspension employed by the Heathen against Christian men and women. If the reader desire to learn more thereanent, let him consult for himself the various authorities and the *Acts* of the Blessed Martyrs already cited. Yet before leaving the subject altogether we will quote one other passage, from St. Gregory Nazianzen, wherein he writes, speaking of St. Mark of Arethusa: "From one crowd of lads to the other he was tossed to and fro, swinging as it were suspended, the boys alternately catching that gallant body on their penknives, and in this tragic wise doing the holy man to death, as it had been some sort of game, . . ." that is to say, the martyr in question was thrown backward and forward between two sets of schoolboys. Many other instances of the same or similar modes of martyrdom might be given, which, however, we be compelled to omit for the sake of brevity.

CHAPTER II

Of the Wheel, the Pulley, and the Press,
as Instruments of Torture

HAVING expounded the divers sorts of hanging, both on Cross and Stake, 'tis only left now to discuss other instruments of torture. But forasmuch as the instruments named above, together with the Wooden Horse, are without doubt the most terrible and appalling of all, we must accordingly treat of them in this place, and of the Horse in the chapter next following. Wherefore, coming to the punishment of the Wheel, which is reputed the most severest penalty of all those mentioned, we note first of all how that this form of torment was practised by the Greeks.

This do we learn from innumerable statements in their own Writers preserved to us,—statements both positive and undisguised. Thus Aristophanes in the *Plutus* saith, "By rights you should be bound to the Wheel, and so forced to reveal your evil doings." Commenting on this same passage, the Scholiast adds, "The Wheel was a contrivance on which slaves were bound down for punishment." Again the same poet, in his *Lysistrata:* "Alackaday ! what a convulsion and a

straining of every limb do I feel! for all the world as though
I were being racked on the Wheel." Anacreon, as quoted
by Athenæus, speaks of the same thing, when he says,
"Many torments and rackings of the neck I endured on the
Wooden Horse, and many on the Wheel." Similarly
Demosthenes (*Oration against Aphobus*): "Let us set Milias
on the Wheel to be tortured;" and Plutarch, in his *Nicias:*
"Then he proceeded to bind the barber to the Wheel, and
further torture him." So Lucian in the *Epistle to Stesichorus*
writes: "After being lopped of their extremities, they were
racked and stretched on Wheels;" and Suidas in his Diction-
ary under the word *Wheel:* "The Wheel was an instrument
of torture for racking men's bodies. Whence Aristophanes:
'Let him be torn on the wheel and flogged.' So slaves were
bound to the Wheel and thrashed. And in another passage:
'You will have to speak up on the Wheel and confess your
crimes.' Thus we see people were tortured on the Wheel and
questioned to discover their complicity with others' and their
own wrong doings. Similarly the Wheel was an apparatus
of wood, on which slaves were bound for punishment." Thus
Suidas.

Phalaris seems to give concurrent testimony in one of
his *Epistles*, where we read: "They were being tortured,
or racked, on the Weeels." Lastly, in confirmation of these
writers, may be appended what is related both by sundry of
the above-quoted authors and by others, concerning Ixion's
being bound to a rolling Wheel, and whirled round for ever
by the same, in just punishment of his offences. The thing

is spoke of by Pindar, Homer (both *Iliad* and *Odyssey*), Lucian, Ovid, Propertius, Seneca, and Claudian.

Other authors there be likewise which make mention of the torture of the Wheel, in especial Josephus, *Maccabees*: "Some refused to eat of polluted meats; these he ordered to be tortured on the Wheel, and put to death;" and again: "For this make ready the wheels, and blow up the fire to a fiercer heat." And again: "But when the Apparitors had set ready the Wheels and Cords, the Tyrant adds," etc.; and, "Then were the Apparitors directed to bring in the elder prisoner; and tearing away his tunic, they bound him hand and foot with thongs every way. And when they which applied the lash were wearied out, without gaining aught, they fixed him about a great Wheel, stretched around the circumference whereof the noble-hearted youth had all his joints dislocated and all his limbs broken." A little further on: "'Wicked hirelings,' cried the youth, 'your Wheel is no more able than you to drown my reason; cut off my limbs, and burn my flesh, and rack my joints with the *twisters*.'[1] On his so saying, they set fire underneath, and divided him limb from limb, stretching his body over the Wheel. And the whole Wheel was stained with his blood, and the grate, which contained the pile of coals, was put out by reason of the drops of blood pouring down upon it, while about the axles of the wheel the gobbets of flesh were carried round and round, the parts adjoining the joints of the bones being

---

[1] *Twisters* (Streblae) were instruments contrived for twisting and dislocating the joints, as in the case of Arthremboles here mentioned.

Fɪɢ. VI.

A. Sometimes Martyrs were bound to the circumference of great wheels, and so hurled from a height over stony places.

everywhere cut to pieces. Nevertheless the high-souled
youth Abraham uttered never a groan, but as if by fire he
were being transformed into incorruption, nobly endured the
twisters, that is the instruments of torment."

And again, "Arthremboles' hands and feet they proceeded
to disarticulate at the joints, and separating these from the
ligaments, tore them away with levers, and so perforated his
fingers, arms, legs and elbows. But when they could in no
wise overcome his resolution, they dragged off the skin together with the tips of the fingers, and instantly led him to the
Wheel, about which were crushed the joints of every limb, and
he saw his own flesh cut to pieces and drops of blood distilled
from his inwards." Also again, "The Apparitors dragged
him bound to the catapults[1]; to which when they had tied
him at the knees, and secured these firmly with iron bands,
they bent back his loins over a rounded wedge, so that all his
body being dashed round the circumference thereof, was
broken in pieces." And a little lower down : "They fastened
him to the Wheel, on which he was stretched and burned with
fire ; moreover they applied spits, sharpened and made red-hot,
to his back, and piercing sides and inwards, seared the
latter."

Thus Josephus, besides whom yet other writers speak of the
Wheel, as Apuleius, *Golden Ass*, "Without an instant's delay,
according to the Greek custom, fire and wheel and every kind

---

[1] *Catapult* generally used to indicate an engine of war used for throwing
arrows, as the Balista was for hurling great stones ; but here means an
instrument of torture.

of torture were exhibited ; " and again, " Neither the Wheel nor the Horse, after the manner of the Greeks, were lacking to his apparatus of torment." Cicero, *Tusculan Orations,* says, " Thus much we are justified in saying, that the happy life cannot end on the Wheel ; " Virgil, *Aeneid,* vi.: " And there they hang, stretched out on the spokes of wheels." Julius Capitolinus : " The Tribune of the Soldiers who allowed his post to be abandoned, this man he tied beneath a wheeled wagon and so dragged him, alive and dead, the whole stage." Again St. Basil, *Homilies on 40 Martyrs,* writes : " Fire moreover was made ready, the sword unsheathed, the cross set up, the sack,[1] the wheel, the scourge prepared ; " and in his *Homily on St. Gordius the Centurion :* " Let his body be torn on the Wheel." Also St. Gregory of Nazianzen and Nicephorus have much to say as to these Wheels. Divers Lives of the Saints likewise speak of them, as in the case of St. Catherine, St. Euphemia, Virgin and Martyr, St. Felix and his companions.

Now these Wheels—as we have clearly gathered from the *Histories* of divers Martyrs—were not of one kind only, but of several. Some, which we find spoke of as *Machines* in the *Acts* of the Saints, were broad and big, while others were narrow. Of both sorts it is our business to treat in this place.

Wherefore as concerning the Wheel of the first sort, of the which Nicephorus and the *Acts* of St. Pantaleëmon speak, be it known how this was contrived in such wise that being taken

---

[1] The *Sack* (Bothrus) identical with the " Culeus " described in a later chapter.

FIG. VII.

A. Martyr whose limbs are interwoven in the spokes of a wheel, on which he is left exposed for days, till he dies.

B. Martyr bound to a narrow wheel, which is revolved, so that his body is horribly mangled on iron spikes fixed underneath.

To face p. 28

up to some high hill, and the victim there bound to its circumference, the Wheel together with the condemned man was
violently hurled down from the summit of the mountain by a
steep and slippery way, so that each several member of the
Martyr's body was broken up. Thus do we read of that most
glorious servant of Christ, Pantaleëmon, in the *History* of his
Martyrdom : "And they said to him, 'Bid the great wheel be
brought, and carried to the top of the mountain, and have him
bound to the said wheel and hurled down the mountain, in
such wise that his flesh may be miserably scattered abroad,
and he give up the spirit.' So the most blessed Pantaleëmon
was led away to prison, while the wheel was a-making. So
soon as it was finished, the Judge ordered the criers to proclaim through the city, that all men should come together for
to see the death of the Blessed Pantaleëmon, and bade him be
brought in. And when the holy Martyr of Christ was led in,
lo ! he was singing psalms to the Lord in Christ. Then the
Attendants holding him, bound him over the wheel ; but as
soon as ever they began to roll the wheel, his bonds were
loosed, and the Holy Martyr stood up unhurt. But the wheel
rolling onward slew sundry among the Heathen." Thus the
Acts of the Saint, wherefrom we learn the truth of what we
have stated as regarding the first kind of Wheels.

There were, moreover, for the massacring of Christians
certain other broad wheels in use among the Heathen, whereof the circumference, to the which the Martyrs were bound, was
provided with blades and sharp nails and the like. To these
wheels, therefore, which hung stationary in the air, the

ministers of iniquity would bind the naked bodies of the Martyrs with cords. Then revolving them along with the wheels again and again with all their might over iron spikes fixed in the earth for piercing and cutting, they caused the flesh of the sufferers thus punished to be torn and mangled in a dreadful fashion. On such a torture wheel we do suppose that Blessed Virgin of Jesus Christ, St. Catherine, to have won the Crown of Martyrdom, as her *Acts* do partly make manifest.

OF WHEELS OF A SECOND SORT.

Other wheels of a lesser breadth than those just described were likewise used by these Devil-worshippers for the torturing of faithful Christians, around the circumference whereof they would very often fix sharp nails and the like, in such wise that their points being turned upward might project beyond the rims. Then on the wheels thus arranged they would bind the Martyrs, whose bodies were pitifully torn by the sharp points of the spikes, as well as by others which stood planted in the earth beneath. In the *Acts* of St. George we find narrated as follows : " Wherefore the Emperor ordered a wheel to be brought in stuck all round with sharp points, and the Saint to be bound naked to the same, and so mangled by the weapons attached thereto. The wheel was hung in the air, while underneath were laid planks, whereon were fixed close together a number of spikes, like sharp swords, some with their points straight upward, others curved like hooks, others resembling flaying knives. Accordingly when the

FIG. VIII.

A. Martyr bound naked to a wheel, which is revolved over iron spikes. | B. Bound to the circumference of a wheel, which is revolved over a fire kindled underneath.

To face p. 30

wheel in its revolutions came near the planks, and the Holy Man, bound like a lamb with slender lines and small cords in such wise that these entered into his flesh and were hid therein, was forced, as the wheel turned, to pass over the swords, his body was caught on their keen edges and sorely lacerated, and contorted and torn in pieces as if with the instrument known as a *scorpion.*" So much for this Saint's death.

It is next to be specially noted how that the Heathen were used, after binding the Martyrs to wheels, then to thrash them cruelly, as they were whirled round on the same, with rods and cudgels. Whereof the *Acts* of St. Clement of Ancyra give testimony in the following terms: "The Magistrate orders the Martyr (that is, Clement) to be bound to the wheel, and the latter to be revolved at great speed, and the Martyr meanwhile to be beaten savagely with rods. And straightway was the Martyr bound to the wheel, and the same turned rapidly. Now the Martyr, when he was atop of the wheel in its revolution, was exposed to the fellows who stood ready with their rods; but when the wheel carried him underneath, then was his body bitterly crushed and his bones broken." Thus the *Acts* of St. Clement, which do manifestly confirm what has been said above.

Further it should be known how that the Heathen were not content for the wreaking of the hate they had conceived against our fellow-Christians with all these sorts of torture, wherewith they bound the Martyrs to wheels and tormented them; but to the same end never ceased to invent new ones.

Hence it came about sometimes that, binding them to wheels having sharp spikes affixed all round, and placed over a fire burning below, they would revolve the same round and round and round at high speed. Wherefore, in just the same fashion as joints on the spit and set to the fire be roasted and cooked, so were these turned about and roasted, that they might become fine bread of Jesus Christ. See the *Acts* of St. Christina, Virgin and Martyr, and of St. Calliopius, wherein you shall find it writ: "'Set up the wheel,' he (the Prefect) said to his Apparitors, 'and kindle a great fire under,' to the which wheel the youth was so tightly bound, as that he was all racked to pieces. Then instantly an Angel of God approached, and put out the flame of the coals; and when the attendants tried to turn the wheel, they could not. But his tender limbs bespattered all the wheel with blood, for it was armed all round with sharp swords." So far the *History* of St. Calliopius. Thus did the Blessed Martyrs, bound to wheels, and carried round with them over a fire, win happily and prosperously and auspiciously the most noble Crown of Martyrdom.

Moreover it was the custom with these same impious men to use the several interstices of the wheels, of the narrow sort above described, in such a way that the limbs of Christ's faithful servants, after being first broke with iron bars, were intertwined and inserted therein so that they appeared, as it were, woven in with the spokes. Then attaching the wheels to the upper end of poles set upright in the ground, they would leave them in this condition to live on for days. This torture, as mentioned by Gregory of Tours (*History of the Franks*), was inflicted at Valence in Gaul upon Felix, a Priest, and Fortunatus and Achilleus, Deacons, the which had been sent thither by St. Irenæus, Bishop of Lyons, to preach the word of God.

It has been abundantly proved in a previous place how that the wheels which (as recorded in sundry *Acts* of the Martyrs) were used for stretching and racking the bodies of Christians, either were pulleys or the wooden horse,—for by means of these instruments, which contained sundry small wheels, and so could be spoke of as wheels, were the bodies of Christ's faithful servants most especially torn,—or else differed in no wise from the wheels just described, as the *History* of St. Calliopius quoted a little above seems clearly to imply. For it states how that he was so straitly bound to the wheel with small cords, that ere ever his tormentors began to revolve it, the blessed youth was mangled and all torn to pieces. Enough said of this most horrible form of torture.

OF PULLEYS.

Pulleys, as instruments of martyrdom, are spoke of by Eusebius in his *Ecclesiastical History*, and in many several *Acts* of the Saints, in especial those of Saints Crispinus and Crispianus, and of St. Quintinus, a Roman citizen. Further mention is made of them by Gregory of Tours (*Hist. of the Franks*), who says : "Stretched at the pulleys, he was beaten with cudgels, rods, and double thongs ; " and again in another place, "He is stretched on the ground at the pulleys, and finally beaten with triple thongs;" and again, "The King was furiously angry and ordered them to be stretched at the pulleys, and violently beaten," etc. Thus Gregory of Tours, a careful study of the chapters quoted from whom will show beyond a doubt that this sort of punishment was especially employed to torture and torment malefactors, scoundrels, and murderers. Wherefore it need cause no surprise if the true worshippers of God, fighting for His honour, were racked or drawn aloft by means of these same pulleys at the hands of the Heathen; for by these were they accounted of all mankind the most wicked and abandoned criminals.

PULLEYS—WHAT WERE THEY?

The Pulley (as is manifest from Vitruvius) was a contrivance for hauling, provided with a roller or little wheel, moving on a small axle, the pulling rope being led over it. It was used either for hoisting weights to a height and into the required positions in building, or for lowering the same, or else for shifting things to and fro, and lastly for drawing water from wells. Now pulleys (see Isidore, *Etymologicum*) are made after the likeness of Θ, the eighth letter of the Greek alphabet, and named *trochleae* from the word *trochla*, which signifies a little wheel. Whence it follows that certain modern writers are in error which hold the *trochlea* (pulley) to have been a capstan or windlass. Granted a pulley is incapable of tearing asunder the bodies of condemned criminals without

FIG. IX.

A. A pulley.

F. Martyrs racked at the pulleys.

C. Crushed in the press, just as grapes and olives are
   pressed in making wine and oil.

D. Capstan or windlass.

To face p. 34

the addition of some special instrument to help, whether a stake to connect it with, or other engine of one sort or another; yet must it not be concluded from this that it *was* a capstan, but only that it required a capstan of some kind. This is our view of the matter. For inasmuch as in this form of torture the bodies of the victims were often horribly stretched and racked, it appears to us proven, especially when we consider the difficulty of tearing a man's body apart, and regard the ease and convenience of the executioners, that some small engine was employed in conjunction with the pulley, viz. a capstan or the like. Read, an you please, the passages of Vitruvius referring to this subject, and you will plainly see that the pulley was not a capstan, nor yet the capstan a pulley. Lastly, we would have you note one thing, to wit that in the accompanying Fig. IX. a capstan is figured along with a pulley, not to imply these were one and the same, but to show the probability that the victims, for the reason just alluded to, were torn and racked by both these instruments at once. We say "probability," because there are other ways in which the same might be done, as very likely it sometimes was.

Now the way wherein Christians were tortured by the pulley was as follows. First of all were fixed in the earth as many stakes as there were victims to be punished. This done, the appointed attendants proceeded to bind the Martyrs, sometimes by their hands, sometimes by their feet, to the ropes of the pulleys one way and to the stakes the other; then the ropes being hauled tight, according to the Judges' orders, their bodies were miserably stretched and racked.   All this is shown in the *Acts* of the sons of St. Symphorosa the Martyr, as also by Gregory of Tours, *History of the Franks*.

You must know further that such as were condemned to this punishment (as is plain from the *History* of the Martyrs, St. Quintinus and St. Ferutius, and sundry passages in Gregory of Tours already noted) at the very same moment they were being racked at the pulleys were simultaneously beaten with cudgels or burned with torches, or else besprinkled with red-hot sulphur and resin, boiling oil, and the like.   Thus in the *Acts* of the Blessed Quintinus these words be found written : "Then the Prefect, raging with despotic fury, orders the holy Quintinus to be so cruelly racked at the pulleys that his limbs were forced to part at the joints from sheer violence.   Moreover, he commanded him to be beaten with small cords, and boiling oil and pitch and melted fat to be poured over his back, that no kind of punishment and torment might fail to add to his bodily anguish.   But when all this failed to content the savage Rictiovarus (such was the Prefect's name) or glut his mad and monstrous thirst for cruelty, he further ordered burning brands to be applied, in such wise that the flames," etc.   Thus the *History* of the blessed Martyr Quintinus.

MARTYRS HOISTED UP WITH PULLEYS.

Lastly we may note how that the Christian martyrs were not only stretched and racked with pulleys, but were likewise hoisted aloft by the same means, in the same fashion wherein

FIG. X.

A. Martyr, with hands tied behind his back, hoisted in the air by a rope.
B. Pulley.

C. Spikes, or sometimes sharp flints, on to which the Martyr was let fall.

To face p. 36

in those times condemned criminals, with hands tied behind their backs, were hauled up in the air by a rope in order to extort the truth from them. This kind of torment is said to have been used with the holy Martyr of Christ, St. Servus, of whom we read in the *Roman Martyrology* under December 7 : "At Tuburbo in Africa, anniversary of the Martyr, St. Servus, who in the Vandal Persecution under King Hunneric, an Arian heretic, was for a long space of time beaten with clubs, then repeatedly hoisted aloft with pulleys, and suddenly let fall again with all the weight of his body on to flint stones. Thus scarified by the sharp stones did he win the palm of martyrdom." So far the *Roman Martyrology ;* further details concerning the same Martyr will be found in Victor, *The Vandal Persecution.*

OF THE PRESS AS AN INSTRUMENT OF TORTURE.

The Christian Martyrs were squeezed in Presses, just in the same way as grapes and olives are pressed therein for to extract wine and oil. By this mode of torture was martyred that most noble soldier of Christ, St. Jonas, of whom we thus read in the *Acts* of the said Martyr: "They (the Persian Magi) ordered the Press to be brought, and St. Jonas to be put therein, and violently pressed and all cut to pieces. The Attendants did as they were commanded, and squeezed him sorely in the Press, and brake all his bones, and finally cut him in twain through the middle."

CHAPTER III

Of the Wooden Horse as an Instrument of Martyrdom; likewise of many and sundry sorts of Bonds

THE Wooden Horse as an instrument of torture is alluded to both by Cicero and by many other Ancient Writers,—by Cicero in the *Pro Deiotaro*, the *Pro Milone,* and the *Philippics.* Other authors which mention the same are Valerius Maximus, Quintilian, Seneca, Ammianus Marcellinus,—likewise innumerable *Histories* and *Acts* of the Martyrs, specially those of St. Crescentianus, Sts. Dorothy, Agatha, and Eulalia, Virgins and Martyrs, Sts. Felix and Fortunatus, Sts. Alexander and Bassus, Bishops and Martyrs,—not to name a countless host of others of either sex.

Beside the Writers and Lives of Saints above referred to, mention is likewise made of the Wooden Horse by St. Cyprian, in his *Epistle to Donatus* and elsewhere, by St. Jerome, St. Augustine, Eusebius, Isidore, and others—as also by Prudentius again and again in his *Hymns.*

All these agree that the Horse was an instrument of torture anciently employed for forcing the truth from suspected or guilty persons. So Cicero, in his *Pro Deiotaro*, writes : " By the custom of our ancestors a slave may bring no charge against his master, even under examination by torture, when pain can force the truth from the most unwilling witness. Yet such was the influence brought to bear on this slave, that the man whom he could not so much as name when on the horse, he openly accuses now he is set free," and again, "To elicit facts, the horse is the proper place ; to discuss points of law, the Court." The same may be gathered from what Ammianus Marcellinus says, "Though he stood bent double under the wooden horse, yet he persisted in a stubborn and uncompromising denial."

Next, the wooden horse was further applied to the purpose of torturing men and racking them cruelly by way of punishment,—as was plainly shown in the case of the Christian martyrs. Accordingly we find frequent mention made of this instrument in the Histories in such continually recurring phrases as,—He was tortured on the horse, Suspended on the horse, Hoisted on to the horse, Put on the horse, and the like.

Now with regard to what we have stated so far, to wit that the wooden horse was a species of torture employed by the Ancients for forcing the truth from accused persons, the divers Writers are all agreed,—but not so concerning its precise description and exact form. For some have declared in so many words that it was a red-hot plate of metal ; others a sort of rack by means of which a man was suspended with hands tied above his head and very heavy weights attached to both feet, and thus cruelly tortured. Others again, Sigonius among the number and many religious authors who have followed him, hold it to have been a sort of wooden framework provided with pulleys and adapted for stretching and again relaxing, intended for torturing people and compelling them to tell the truth about some circumstance. "Now the nature of this torture," he says, "was as follows. After binding to this frame the arms and legs of the person to be tortured by means of small thongs known as fiddle strings, they then extended the said framework and set it upright, so that the victim found himself suspended on it, as on a cross. This done, they proceeded in the first place to drag asunder all the joints and articulations of his limbs ; then putting red-hot plates close to his body, and last of all tearing his sides with two-pronged iron hooks, they by these means increased the bitterness of his torment yet further." So far the most learned Sigonius.

On the contrary, others maintain that it was merely a wooden contrivance fashioned something like a horse (as we shall explain at length further on), having two channelled wheels, or pulleys, fixed at either end in hollows made to receive them, and capable of being revolved by their pins or axles. Over these ropes were led in such a way that accused persons could be fastened to them, and so tortured in various ways and racked and stretched.

Such are the divers opinions held by divers writers concerning the wooden horse, the truth or falsity whereof will readily be made manifest, if the matter be looked into with proper pains.

Now, if we consider the first of these, we shall undoubtedly find it less agreeable to truth than any of the others. For how can we suppose the "horse" itself to have been a red-hot plate, when we read in almost any History of the Martyrs, as well as in sundry works of Ancient authors, of men being hoisted on the horse and there burned with red-hot plates? Coming next to the second and third views, we shall be able to prove easily and conclusively the unlikelihood of these and their discrepancy with the truth. For in what way can the facts our predecessors have stated in their writings about the wooden horse be made to accord with these accounts? It is an impossibility; and indeed we shall be in a position to prove by sufficient reasons that the last quoted opinion, which we hold to be the true one, is actually so. This view may be restated for the sake of clearness thus :—

The "horse" among the Ancients was an engine of wood fashioned to resemble a real horse, and having two small, channelled wheels, or pulleys, in the two ends, which were hollowed out to receive them. Over the axles of these, when anyone was to be tortured on the instrument, ropes were led, and the wheels revolved, by which means the person tied to them was racked and stretched in divers directions.

But to make clearer and plainer yet both what we said above and the further explanations we have just added, it should be known what course the Ancients pursued in the making of an "horse." To begin with, they did prepare a straight beam of wood of a convenient length and breadth; into the two ends of this, which they had previously had somewhat hollowed out, they affixed small channelled wheels, turning on wheels or axles; then to the end the whole thing might be raised clear above the ground, they chose four other pieces of timber shorter and thinner than the first, which they fastened with iron nails near the four several corners, so completing an engine standing on four legs and something resembling a real horse. When all was ready, if there was any to be racked on the horse, his two legs were drawn forcibly apart, and he was clapped on its back. Then the tormentors took ropes, with one of which they tied the man's feet, and with the other his hands, after they had twisted the latter behind him. Next, leading these ropes over the small wheels or pulleys and carrying them to a little contrivance of the nature of a winch or windlass (as may be conjectured) affixed to the horse's legs, winding the ropes about this and turning it round, they drew the bonds taut in such wise that the man, tied with his back to the horse's back and his face looking skywards, was stretched along with them. Thus they would continue turning unweariedly, drawing the ropes tighter and tighter, till every limb was strained and every joint dislocated. After some long while they would either leave him so, or else at a sign from the Judge relax the ropes and let him drop and so hang bent under the horse's belly, to his sore anguish. Then the Judge, deeming he had now gotten a good occasion either for convicting or acquitting the prisoner, would proceed to question and cross-question him straitly of his doings. But an if the victim's firmness held out and cheated the magistrate of his expectation, he would now order hot plates to be fetched, or else iron claws and hooks and the like, to the end this fresh aggravation of his pain might yet elicit the truth.

FIG. XI.

A. Martyr on the wooden horse.
B. Martyr hanging from the horse.
C. The wooden horse.

D. Consular fasces.
E. Platform or scaffold whereon the wooden horse was fixed.

To face p. 42

Of the Wooden Horse

So much for the shape and way of using of the wooden horse ; it is only left now to confirm the explanation we have given in each and every particular by other considerations and the evidence of Ancient authors.

In the first place, that this engine of wood was made in the likeness of a real horse is manifest from the very name given it of *horse* (*equuleus*). Moreover, to this day divers sorts of benches and other articles of furniture that be raised somewhat from the ground on four legs are called "horses." Again, the language employed by sundry Ancient writers shows clearly that in speaking of prisoners being set on the wooden instrument, they had in their mind's eye the mounting of actual, live horses. Thus Cicero, in the *Tusculan Orations*, "They mount the wooden horse," "Trying to get on the horse's back." So again the poet Pomponius writes : "And when I had leapt" (a word properly used of anyone mounting a horse) "on the back of the pulley horse, I was tortured full-trot,"—after mounting the horse with the channelled wheels, I was tortured at a great pace, that is to say, by means of the ropes and pulleys provided for that purpose. So too we read constantly in descriptions of the Blessed Martyrs' sufferings, particularly in that of Saints Abundius and Abundantius, how the Christians were hoisted on the horse to be tortured. It is perfectly plain, then, that the horse (as already said) was an engine of wood made in the likeness of a horse, and nothing else whatever.

Lastly, this view would seem to be greatly corroborated by St. Jerome, *Epistle to the Innocents*, and Seneca, of whom the former writes that persons tortured on the wooden horse kept their eyes turned heavenwards, the latter that they lay extended full length on it. Thus St. Jerome says, "Albeit his body was stretched upon the horse, his eyes,—the only part of him the tormentor could not bind,—gazed up to heaven;" and Seneca, "You actually try to persuade us it makes no matter whether a man be in joyful case or be lying on the horse." If therefore, as is here said, prisoners lay on the wooden horse and looked up to heaven, it is more likely this instrument was fashioned like a horse than otherwise.

Again, the fact that the horse was fitted with little channelled wheels, or pulleys, may be concluded from the verses of the ancient poet Pomponius already quoted, as manifestly appears from the facts and explanations we have given above.

Again, that victims were hoisted up on the horse, with arms twisted behind back and legs bound to the engine with cords, which were led over certain little contrivances in the nature of pulleys, and so stretched and torn asunder, this, I repeat, may be proved from many and sundry passages, and particularly from Eusebius' *History,* where these words are found : "For in the first place certain were suspended with hands tied behind them to the wood, and by means of certain engines all their limbs stretched and strained asunder, etc." Further, that this is to be understood of the wooden horse, the passage which immediately follows seems to show plainly enough. Next, at the magistrates' command were they sorely racked in their whole body by the tormentors, and not only their sides, as is commonly done with murderers, but their belly also and shins and knees were beaten with iron scourges or claws." Moreover the evidence can be yet further strengthened by another passage from St. Jerome's *Epistle to the Innocents*, where it is writ, "But indeed the woman was stronger than her sex, and albeit the horse was racking her body, while her hands stained with the filth of the prison were bound with cords behind her, yet with her eyes," etc.

The same may be gathered from Prudentius' Hymn on the Martyrdom of St. Vincent, in which the Tyrant thus addresses the tormentors :—

> *Vinctum retortis brachiis*
> *Sursum et deorsum extendite,*
> *Compago donec ossium*
> *Divulsa membratim crepet.*

("Go bind the man with arms twisted behind the back, and rack him up and down, till the framework of his bones crack, as he is torn limb from limb.") And again from that for St. Romanus' day, where the indomitable Martyr speaks thus from the horse's back :—

> *Miserum putatis, quod retortis pendeo*
> *Extensus ulnis, quod revelluntur pedes,*
> *Compago nervis quod sonat crepantibus.*

("You deem me unhappy, because I hang stretched here with elbows twisted behind me, because my legs are drawn asunder and all my frame cracks as the sinews are racked.")

From all these passages it plainly follows, in our opinion,

that prisoners were bound hand and foot with cords, the hands being twisted behind the back, and by the revolution of certain little contrivances to which the ropes were led, were racked limb by limb and torn asunder.

That the horse was provided with contrivances of the nature of pulleys, not to appeal again to the evidence adduced already from Eusebius, may be further corroborated from what Vitruvius the architect says in his Works when treating of the use of pulleys and other instruments for hauling, such as the capstan and windlass. He lays it down that a running rope after being led over a pulley must, if weights are to be lifted or shifted, be carried eventually to some engine of the windlass kind.

The fact that victims lay stretched full length on the horse with face turned upward, whilst the ropes were being hauled taut, is shown manifestly enough by the passages quoted from St. Jerome and Seneca ; but there is one other point should be noted (as we are advised by this same Epistle of St. Jerome), to wit, that the executioners were sometimes used, by way of further increasing the torment, to fasten the hair of women undergoing the punishment of the horse to the wood thereof. And no wonder this was an aggravation of the pain, for whereas the ropes were slackened by the tormentors, and the victims fell under the horse's belly (as will be shown presently from Ammianus Marcellinus) with bodies hanging bent in a curve, the hair was bound to be strained and dragged out of the scalp, to the extreme and excessive torment both of mind and body.

But as to the victims falling underneath the instrument with bodies hanging bent when the tightened ropes were slackened, this fact is attested, amongst other authors, by Ammianus Marcellinus, who writes, "He delivered up many innocent persons to the tormentors, and put them to hang with bodies bent underneath the horse," and again (as already quoted), "Albeit he stood with his body bent underneath the horse, yet did he persist in a stubborn and uncompromising denial." Now in these passages, and particularly the latter, did the author mean to imply that the ropes were slackened in order to increase the pain, or for the sake of diminishing and relieving the same? The first is our own opinion, whereas the second is maintained by Sigonius and his followers. He holds that the Ancients were used to relax the ropes, whereby the bodies of prisoners were stretched on the horse, for the purpose of relieving the pain. Accordingly he writes, "Even as the horse, or rather the strings thereof were drawn tight in order to excite pain, so were these relaxed again for to relieve the same,"—quoting, to confirm his opinion by the authority of the Ancients, the following from Valerius Maximus, "Whenas Zeno was being tortured by Nearchus the Tyrant, he declared there was something it much behoved the other to hear privily ; then when the horse was slackened, he did catch the tyrant's ear betwixt his teeth and bit it off;" and again in another place, "Hieronymus the Tyrant exhausted the efforts of the tormentors in vain; for he brake the scourges, loosened the cords, relaxed the horse and put out the red-hot plates, before he could compel the other to reveal his confederates in tyrannicide."

Another point we would have the reader note,—this slackening of the ropes (as is shown in the passage just quoted from Valerius Maximus) clearly implies the fact, which we stated at the beginning of the chapter, that the wooden horse was raised somewhat from the ground in all parts. Wherefore we need not be surprised if Prudentius, in his Hymn on the Martyrdom of St. Romanus, represents that soldier of Christ as crying out from the horse, as from the top of an elevated structure :

Audite cuncti : clamo longe, ac praedico,
Emitto vocem de catasta celsior,

("Hear, all men : I cry aloud and proclaim my tidings, I utter my voice, lifted high on this scaffold.")

But enough said on this part of our subject.

"FIDICULAE"—WHAT DID THE ANCIENTS MEAN BY THE WORD ?

Sigonius in the passage quoted just above states his opinion that these were the thongs or bands whereby the prisoner's limbs were bound to the wooden horse, and that to speak of criminals as being tortured with the *fidiculae* is the same thing as saying they were attached by these thongs to the horse, and thereafter all the joints of their bones stretched and dragged asunder to their extreme dolour. But there are divers considerations convince us beyond a doubt that the scholars which hold this view be quite mistaken ; and fully to satisfy the indulgent reader on this point, we do propose to set these forth here at length.

St. Isidore doth declare with the utmost exactness that

they were not thongs at all, but rather iron claws or hooks wherewith such as were condemned to torture were lacerated. This again agreeth with what Prudentius says in his Hymn of St. Romanus the Martyr, where he speaks of *fidiculae* as if they were a sort of claws or hooks. These are the words he puts in the mouth of Asclepias the Judge :—

> *Vertat ictum carnifex*
> *In os loquentis, inque maxillas manuum,*
> *Sulcosque acutos, et fidiculas transferat,*
> *Verbositatis ut rumpatur locus.*

("Let the executioner aim a blow at the speaker's lips, and harass his jaws with sharp cuts and *iron claws*, to the end the place wherefrom words come may be destroyed.") That by *fidiculae* here Asclepias meant claws, is made manifest by the verses the author immediately subjoins :—

> *Implet jubentis dicta lictor improbus,*
> *Charaxat ambas ungulis scribentibus*
> *Genas, cruentis et secat faciem rotis :*
> *Hirsuta barbis solvitur carptim cutis,*
> *Et mentum adusque vultus omnis scinditur.*

("The cruel lictor obeys the Judge's orders ; he marks both his cheeks with the writing of the iron claws, and ploughs his face with bloodstained wheels. The skin and the beard that roughens it are flayed away in patches, the chin and all the features lacerated.") So far Prudentius.

On the other hand, Suetonius (*Tiberius*) seems to go against this view in a passage where *fidiculae* are spoken of apparently as quite a different form of punishment : " He had devised yet another mode of torture; after treacherously inducing his victims to drink long and heavily, he would suddenly have their privates tied up, so that they suffered agonies both from the constriction of the strings (*fidiculae*) and the distension of their bladders by the accumulated urine." This is what Suetonius says; but without disputing his authority, it may be at once admitted that here we have something altogether different from what is recorded as to *fidiculae* in the Histories of the Blessed Martyrs and the other authorities quoted. But enough of this.

However, with regard to what we said above concerning certain other kinds of tortures, in which prisoners were stretched on the wooden horse and tormented, it should be noted that our ancestors had the habit of stretching a person on that instrument, and then by means of *fidiculae* or iron claws tearing his limbs, or else burning the same with red-hot plates of metal, or the like. This is to be found recorded in sundry collections of *Acts* of the Blessed Martyrs, and particularly in St. Cyprian's *Epistle to Donatus*, where he writes: "The spear was there, and the sword, and the executioner standing ready, the iron claw that mangles and scrapes the sides, the horse that stretches the limbs, and the fire that burns,—many kinds of torments for one poor human body!" And again in another place: "But anon the hard-hearted Judge's cruelty was roused afresh, and the victim, already worn out with pain, was again torn by the lash, beaten by the cudgels, racked on the horse, lacerated by the iron claw and scorched by the flames." So too St. Augustine also writes in his *Epistle to Marcellinus:* "When, I ask, did you drag forth confession of such heinous crimes, not by the horse that stretches the limbs, nor the iron claws that mangle or the flames that burn, but by mere blows of the lash?" Likewise Cicero, *In Verrem:* "But what when fire and red-hot plates and the rest of the torturer's contrivances were brought in?" and in the *Philippics:* "Call up before your eyes bonds and lashes, the horse, the executioner, and grim Samarius the torturer." Similarly Seneca: "And all his apparatus of cruelty must be paid back to him, his horses and his iron claws, his fetters and crosses, his stakes and fires, and the hook that drags the mangled corpse from the arena;" and Ammianus Marcellinus: "The horses were stretched ready, and the executioner was fitting his hooks and preparing his instruments of torture." It only remains to quote a few verses from the Hymns of Prudentius illustrating the same subject. From the Hymn of St. Vincent, Martyr :—

> *Extorque, si potes, fidem.*
> *Tormenta, carcer, ungulae,*
> *Stridensque flammis lamina,*
> *Atque ipsa poenarum ultima*
> *Mors Christianis ludus est.*

And a little further on in the same :

> *Ridebat haec miles Dei,*
> *Manus cruentas increpans*
> *Quod fixa non profundius*
> *Intraret artus ungula.*

("Rob me of my faith, an if you can. Tortures, prison, iron claws, the red-hot plate crackling with flames, and death itself, the last of punishments, all are but sport to Christian men;" "All this God's champion made mock of, clapping his bleeding hands, laughing because the hook that pierced his flesh ate not more deeply in.")

Likewise from the Hymn of St. Romanus, the Martyr :—

> *Amor coronae poenae praevenit trucem*
> *Lictoris artem, sponte nudas offerens*
> *Costas bisulcis execandas ungulis.*

And again in the same :—

> *Non ungularum tanta vis latus fodit*
> *Mucrone, quanta dira pulsat pleuresis :*
> *Nec sic inusta laminis ardet cutis,*
> *Ut febris atro fele venas exedit.*

(" Love of the crown of martyrdom forestalls the savage skill of the torturer, willingly offering naked flanks to be lacerated by the two-pronged hooks ;" "Not so sharp do the iron claws tear the side with their keen points, as pleurisy does when it makes its dread attack ; not so hot the fiery plates burn and scorch the skin, as fever and black bile when they consume the veins.")

From all these passages, therefore, it doth very manifestly appear that the view we have ourselves adopted and declared concerning the horse is the true one, to wit that this was an engine of wood wrought in the likeness of a real horse ; and not as Sigonius would have it, a sort of scaffold merely or platform. For, if it were the latter, how could the poet Pomponius, as cited above, have spoke of prisoners *leaping on the horse,* and Cicero have used words of a like implication? Or how could Ammianus Marcellinus have described men being racked on the horse, and then when the ropes wherewith they were bound were slackened, immediately falling underneath the same with the body hanging bent in a curve and not extended straight?

But to come to Sigonius' alleged reasons and the refutation thereof. His first point is that Eusebius (*Ecclesiastical History*), making mention of the horse, doth imply it was some sort of scaffold or platform of wood that was generally used to be raised aloft. His words are: "But when these cruel and tyrannical forms of torture, by reason of the Saints' holy patience, which was confirmed by Christ's merits, seemed to have been appealed to and inflicted all in vain, the devil did devise certain other fresh contrivances against them. Wherefore were they thrown into dungeons, and lay miserably, in places dark and gloomy and full of every horror, while sometimes their feet were fixed in heavy stocks and stretched wide apart even as far as the fifth hole." This shows the horse, Sigonius adds, to have been a wooden platform, on which the bodies of criminals were stretched. Other passages he relies on are from Sozomen (*History*), where, speaking of Busiris, a Christian from the Galatian town of Ancyra who was crucified for the Faith at Myros, a city of Phrygia, under the Emperor Julian the Apostate, he writes thus: "So when they had brought him to the beam of torment, he ordered this to be raised aloft," and again, "From among the Christians which had been cast into prison he selects first a young man named Theodore, and binds him to the stake on which punishments were usually inflicted, where he was mangled with iron claws for a long while. Similarly Prudentius—not to quote a second time the verses from his Hymn on the martyrdom of St. Romanus, where he makes that Saint speak of *uttering his voice from on high on the scaffold*— says of a martyr :—

> *" Scindunt utrumque milites teterrimi*
> *Mucrone bisulco pensilis latus viri."*

("The savage soldiers cut open with a two-edged sword either side of the man as he hung there.")

Such then be the main arguments whereto Sigonius and they that follow his opinion do trust, the which we have now to refute ; and to make the said refuting an easier matter, we must declare to begin with that this scholar hath manifestly made a confusion betwixt the wooden horse on the one hand, and on the other, firstly, the wooden platform or scaffold whereon criminals were used to be set to be tortured, and secondly, with the heavy fetters or stocks wherein prisoners in gaol had their legs fixed and stretched asunder to the fourth or fifth hole, and so kept in constant pain.

Moreover it may be noted by the way how that this word *platform* hath yet another meaning, signifying sometimes, though less properly, a contrivance like a long and large set of stocks wherein slaves were kept shackled when exposed for sale ; again, that it is used on occasions to mean the frame or gridiron whereon St. Lawrence and other martyrs died. So Prudentius, in his Hymn on St. Lawrence, sings :—

Of the Wooden Horse

Postquam vapor diutius
Decoxit exustum latus,
Ultro ex catasta Judicem
Compellat affatu brevi :
Converte partem corporis,
Satis crematus jugiter.

("Whenas the heat had long been scorching and roasting the one side, accosting the Judge from the frame—that is from the iron gridiron—the Martyr quoth shortly and briefly : Turn my body now o' the other side ; this one is burned enough and to spare.") But it is obvious that the true and general meaning of this word *platform* or *scaffold* was a raised place whereon folk were lifted up to the end their tortures might be better seen by those present, and that in his expounding of the word *horse*, our scholar hath confused these two things together.

One word more concerning that sort of shackles or stocks wherein prisoners were set in gaol, their legs parted to the fourth or fifth hole, and so kept for long and continued torment. This instrument can in no wise be the same with the wooden horse, as hath been maintained, for divers reasons. First, because by the operation of the former men were made broader, whereas by the latter, as we do find it stated in Seneca, longer. Secondly, it is plain this former sort of punishment was only used in the gaol (as will be made yet more manifest presently, when we come to treat of bonds and fetters), but the latter on the contrary, as countless *Acts* of the Blessed Martyrs do bear witness, outside the prison walls, and most generally in the public places of cities. Thirdly, on the horse not alone the legs of the victim were racked and stretched

ready for the mangling by the iron claws, but the whole body
likewise, whereas in the stocks the legs only were drawn
asunder. All this showeth these were something entirely
different from the wooden horse.

OF MANY DIVERS WAYS WHEREIN THE BODIES OF PRISONERS WERE RACKED AND STRETCHED.

Further we must understand it was the custom of the
Ancients to rack and stretch the bodies of persons accused
in sundry ways, to wit by means of the horse, by pulleys, or
by hanging up with heavy weights attached to the feet—as
also to torture the same with divers and sundry other torments,
such as mangling with claws and iron combs and other similar
instruments, or burning with red-hot plates and the like. And
these same tortures were effected in divers fashions, either by
hoisting the victims on the wooden horse, or suspending them
in any of the different ways described above in Chapter I., by
tying of them up whether to stakes or trees or pillars.

OF THE FASHIONS WHEREIN FOLK WERE BOUND TO THE WOODEN HORSE, AND HOW THEY WERE SUSPENDED THEREFROM AS FROM AN ELEVATED BEAM ; LIKEWISE OF THE TRUE SIGNIFICATION OF BEING HANGED ON THE HORSE.

Again and again we read in accounts of the passion of the
Blessed Martyrs words of this sort : " The Martyr was hanged
on horse,"—from the which fashion of speech many have
assumed (as said above) that the *horse* was not framed to

resemble a real horse, but was something different. Surely these have not considered a fact plainly proven from the works of Ancient authors, to wit that this word *hanged* doth also signify simply to be raised or lifted up to any place,—a thing they could not but have noted, had they read their books with any care. To speak, then, of a Martyr's being hanged on the horse is the same thing as to say he was lifted up thereon. Hence it is that in reading the Histories of the Saints which have won the Crown of Martyrdom, we find assigned to the Judge or Emperor who is ordering someone to be tortured on the horse such words as these : " Let the man be hoisted on the horse, and there racked." Thus in the *Acts* of the most Blessed Saints Abundius, Priest, and Abundantius, Deacon, it is related : "Then Diocletian commanded them to be hoisted on the horse and tortured for a long space of time ; and when they were being so tortured," etc. To be hanged on the horse, then, means nothing more nor less than simply to be lifted up on the same.

This is confirmed likewise by the *Histories* of Sts. Regina and Marguerite, Virgins and Martyrs, at the beginning of which it is writ, " Marguerite was hanged on the horse," while a little further down it is added, "After many days the folk again came together and she is brought before the Judge, and scorning to make sacrifice to idols, she is again hoisted on the horse," etc.

Lastly, we may add that on occasion the martyrs did actually hang suspended from the horse to which they were bound. For when the ropes wherewith they were tied were slackened, they would fall underneath the horse's belly with bodies bent in a curve. Thus they hung not straight down from the instrument, as persons hanged do usually, but (as stated above) with bodies bent underneath it—a fact abundantly testified by Ammianus Marcellinus in sundry passages already quoted.

OF STRETCHING OR EXTENDING THE WOODEN HORSE.

Mention is sometimes found in Ammianus and sundry other writers of the horse being wont to be stretched and again relaxed. This of course is to be understood not of the engine itself, but of the ropes wherewith the victim to be tortured was bound thereto, forasmuch as when these were drawn tight or slackened, the horse itself appeared in a way to be extended and again relaxed.

WHY THE WOODEN HORSE WAS CALLED A POST, AND WHY A CROSS, EXPOUNDED.

The fabric of the wooden horse (as already stated) was formed of an oblong post or baulk of timber, supported on four other pieces or legs. This is referred to by St. Jerome, *Epistle to the Innocents*, in these words : " Her hair is fastened to the post, and her whole body bound to the horse ; then is a fire brought near her feet, and at the same moment the executioner tears both her sides," etc. In the same way Prudentius speaks of the whole fabric of the horse as the *accursed post* in his hymn of St. Romanus the Martyr, where he says :—

Incensus his Asclepiades jusserat
Eviscerandum corpus equuleo eminus
Pendere, et uncis ungulisque crescere.

And a few lines further down :—

Jubet amoveri noxialem stipitem
Plebeia clara poena ne damnet virum.

("Angered by the words, Asclepiades had ordered his body to hang aloft for to be mangled on the horse, and to endure the hooks and iron claws." "He commands the accursed post to be removed, to save the noble victim from so plebeian a doom.")

Nor is this the only other name given the wooden horse, for we find it likewise called *mala mansio,* or "bad quarters." Again, it is sometimes spoke of as a *cross;* thus in the *Acts* of St. Dorothy, Virgin and Martyr, among the holy days of the month of February, these words are writ concerning a certain Theophilus which was tortured on the wooden horse, "Now behold! I am a Christian; for have I not been hanged upon the cross,—that is to say the wooden horse? For this same horse hath a certain likeness to the cross."

And indeed 'tis no wonder it was so called, for in the first place we do read of other sorts of instruments of torture being likewise called crosses; secondly, because the bodies of them that were afflicted thereon were used to be stretched out like those of persons crucified; thirdly and lastly, because the wooden posts which represented the horse's legs, besides being nailed to the main timber, were likewise joined to one another and connected by cross pieces, albeit they were wide apart nearer the ground, whence it was that each pair of posts did form as it were the two arms of a cross.

One more quotation, and enough will have been said on this part of our subject. Sozomen, speaking of a certain Christian named Busiris, writes, "So taking him to the public place where the wooden horse was, he orders him to be hanged up aloft thereon. Whereupon Busiris, lifting his hands to his head, did strip bare his own sides, and addressing the Governor, said there was no call for the lictors to take needless pains in lifting him up on to the horse and again removing him therefrom to the ground," etc.—a passage which doth yet further corroborate our former words as to what the wooden horse really was, to wit, an engine made in the likeness of a live horse, whereon the Martyrs were lifted up to be tortured, and not a mere platform or scaffold.

OF THE STOCKS, AND DIVERS OTHER FASHIONS OF BINDING PRISONERS FAST.

A little above we did distinguish the wooden horse from the stocks, wherein Martyrs were kept in torment with their legs forced asunder to the fourth or fifth hole. Now it behoves us to note how that among the Ancients were divers sorts of bonds in use, to wit, the stocks, thongs, chains, shackles, fetters, manacles, neck collars, and the gaol. These Plautus doth enumerate in his play, the *Asinaria* :—

> *Advorsum stimulos, laminas, crucesque, compedesque,*
> *Nervos, catenas, carceres, numellas, pedicas, boias.*

("Against scourges and red-hot plates, against the cross and the stocks, against thongs, chains, prisons, shackles, fetters, and neck collars.")

OF THE STOCKS.

The stocks was a wooden contrivance, wherein the legs of prisoners and criminals were used to be constrained, constricted, and confined. Both Plautus and Terence, among Ancient writers, make mention thereof—the former author in the *Captivi,* where he says :—

Ubi ponderosas crassas capiat compedes

("When he is set in the heavy ponderous stocks "); the latter in the *Phormio :—*

Molendum usque in pistrino, vapulandum, habendae compedes

("We must grind for ever in the mill, and be beat, and endure the stocks ").

Horace again hath something to say on the subject in his *Epodes :—*

*Ibericis peruste funibus latus
Et crura dura compede.*

("You whose side is chafed with Iberian bonds, and your legs galled by the rough timbers of the stocks.")

And again in the *Epistles :—*

*. . . Argentum tollas licet, in manicis et
Compedibus salvo te sub custode tenebo.*

("Yes! you may take the money, but I will keep you manacled and in the stocks under a hard taskmaster.")

In this sort of stocks were the Blessed Martyrs cruelly

tormented; for (as we are informed in passages quoted a little above) after scourging and scarifying with iron claws, their legs were stretched and forcibly drawn apart even to the fourth or fifth hole of the instrument. Of this Prudentius speaks in one of his Hymns :—

> *In hoc barathrum conjicit*
> *Truculentus hostis martyrem,*
> *Lignoque plantas inserit,*
> *Divaricatis cruribus.*

("Into this dungeon the truculent tyrant throws the martyr, and, forcing his legs asunder, inserts his feet in the stocks.") It seems likewise from what Eusebius saith that when so set in the stocks, they were necessarily compelled to lie flat on their backs on a wooden board. He writes : "Some, moreover, after scourging were set in the stocks and their legs forced one from the other as far as four holes apart, in such wise that they were necessarily compelled to lie on their back on the wood, albeit they could not do so without sore difficulty, seeing their whole bodies were covered with fresh wounds inflicted by the lash." So much for the stocks.

THE SHACKLES.

These too are mentioned in the lines just quoted from the *Asinaria* of Plautus; and thus described by Nonius : "The shackle is a species of wooden contrivance formerly employed for torturing criminals by the Ancients, the victim's neck and feet being both inserted therein;" that is to say, it was a wooden instrument with round holes, into which the feet and neck of prisoners were inserted, and fixed there in such a way that they could not withdraw them again.

Our own belief, however, is that this word *shackle* was used by the Ancients to signify several different sorts of bonds, a conclusion we are led to by the words of Sextus Pompeius, who speaks thereof in these terms : "The shackle is a sort of bond or fastening wherewith four-footed beasts are secured; it is made of a thong or a strip of raw ox-hide, as a general rule." This differs from Nonius' account, so that, unless we be prepared to say outright that one of the twain was mistaken, we cannot but conclude the word to have been applied in two different meanings.

OF THONGS.

These are mentioned by Plautus in the *Captivi* :—

Nam noctu nervo vinctus custodibitur

("For at night-time he shall be kept guarded and bound with a thong ") ; in the *Curculio* :—

Atque ita te nervo torquebo, ibidem ut catapultae solent

("And I will wrench your limbs with a thong, even as the catapults are used to do "); and in many other passages to boot. Likewise St. Cyprian, *Epistles to Clergy and People*, says, speaking of Celerinus : "For nineteen days he was shut up in prison, bound with thongs and iron bands. . . ."

But Sextus Pompeius adds something more in his description thereof, saying, "We likewise give this name to an iron fetter for the feet, though Plautus speaks of it as used also for the neck." From all which we may gather the following definition : "A thong is a species of bond used for securing the feet or neck." Hence the saying of Cato recorded by Aulus Gellius : "Thieves guilty of private thefts pass their days in confinement by thong and fetters, public robbers in purple and gold."

OF FETTERS.

Fetters were snares or nooses wherewith the feet of prisoners or criminals were secured, being so called because they confine the feet, just as manacles, or handcuffs, are so called because they imprison the hands.

OF MANACLES.

Manacles are bands for the hands ; as the Psalm saith : "For binding their kings in fetters and their princes in bands of iron." Plautus again in his *Mostellaria* writes :—

> *Ut cum extemplo vocem,*
> *Continuo exiliatis, manicas celeriter connectite*

("So that the moment I call, you may instantly spring forth ; then quickly fasten the manacles together ") ; and in the *Captivi* :— *Injicite huic actutum manicas mastigiae*

("Go, put manacles instantly on this scoundrel here "). Also Virgil in the Second *Aeneid* :—

> *Ipse viro primus manicas, atque arcta levari*
> *Vincla jubet Priamus*

("King Priam himself is the first to bid release the man from

64

his manacles and constraining bonds ")—not to mention a number of other authors, whom, for the sake of brevity, we must refrain from quoting.

The English heretics at this present moment (1591) are busied unceasingly in malignantly and cruelly afflicting them of the orthodox faith by means of iron manacles, or handcuffs as they call them. These are a sort of instrument whereby a man is hung up and tortured, his two hands being put through an iron ring toothed inside, and violently squeezed. Indeed, so fierce and intense is the pain that unless the back is allowed to lean somewhat against a wall and the tips of the toes to touch the floor, the man will fall incontinently into a dead faint. If you would learn more of these atrocities, read Father Sanders' Work on the *Anglican Schism*, wherein the author doth call this kind of torture the *iron gauntlets*.—But enough of this ; so now to proceed to other matters.

OF NECK-COLLARS.

These may be described as follows : " Neck-collars were a sort of necklace or neck-band for condemned criminals, made either of wood or iron, which imprisoned their necks firmly, as the yoke doth with oxen." In addition to these we opine there were other sorts of neck-collars likewise, differing from these, yet of the same nature, and called generally collars, which Nonius thus defines, "The collar is any sort of bond whereby the neck is constrained." So in Lucilius we find, "That with manacles, leash, and collar, I may fetch home the fugitive." Indeed these neck-collars, as is plainly shown in the *Acts* of St. Balbina and of Pope Alexander, were largely employed among men of earlier days for binding and making fast the necks of prisoners and criminals. So we read, "Anon, kissing the neck-collars of the most glorious Martyr, Pope Alexander, that Blessed Martyr of Christ, St. Balbina, heard these words pronounced : 'Cease, daughter, to salute these collars, and go seek instead the bonds of my master, St. Peter . . .'" Hence it would seem these last were something of the same nature ; and indeed when the bonds, preserved to this day in the Church of St. Peter ad Vincula at Rome, wherewith that Holy Apostle of Christ was bound, be examined, they will be found to include a round iron collar for the securing of the Martyr's neck.

OF CHAINS.

A *chain* is an iron bond wherewith slaves or prisoners are made fast to hinder their escaping. Thus Livy the Historian, writing of the first years after the foundation of Rome, "Turnus awaking from sleep finds himself surrounded by guards. His slaves were seized, who for love of their master were preparing to resist, swords being produced from all corners of the refuge. There could be no longer any doubt, and Turnus was loaded with chains ;" also Cicero, *In Verrem*, "The miscreant orders chains to be bound upon unfortunate and innocent men "—beside very many other writers which make the like reference.

Moreover we read again and again in the *Acts* of the Saints how in the days of persecution the Christians were bound with iron chains, as is attested, amongst others, by the *History* of St. Anastasia, a Roman Martyr, Saint Febronia, Virgin and Martyr, St. Chrysanthus, and a host of other Saints and Martyrs of either sex.

Further, if any desire to learn in what fashion prisoners were bound with chains in Antiquity, let him go look at the figures to be seen to this day carved and cut on the Arch of the Emperor Constantine. There he will see a number of captives so confined.

OF PRISONS OR GAOLS.

A *prison* or *gaol* is a place wherein criminals are kept guarded, and from which no man can go forth of his own free will. The first prison at Rome was built by King Ancus Martius, by what Livy tells us, "Likewise the pit or dungeon of the Quirites, no insignificant monument as viewed from the more level ground, is the work of King Ancus. The state having largely increased in prosperity, and, as was to be expected with so numerous a population, the distinctions of right and wrong being grown confused and crimes of fraud and stealth become frequent, a gaol is built to overawe the increasing lawlessness, in the midmost of the city, looking over the forum itself."

Now it should be observed there were two divers fashions of guarding prisoners among the Ancients, to wit, the public gaol and the private house. To the latter they were used to deliver over accused persons previous to their confession or conviction. This was spoke of as *free custody*, when persons were entrusted to the custody of magistrates at their own house, or to that of private noblemen. Thus Livy, speaking of the Judge of the Bacchanalia, doth write : "The Consul begs his father-in-law to clear a part of his house, that Hispala might be lodged there," etc. Then, a few lines further on, "The Consuls ordered the Curule Ædiles to seek out all his priests, arrest them, and keep them for future examination in free confinement." The same thing again is implied in what Sallust says, writing of the Catilinarian conspiracy : "The Senate decreed that the Magistracy be abolished, and Lentulus and the rest of the confederates be kept in free custody. Accordingly Lentulus was delivered over to Publius Lentulus Spinther, who was Ædile at the time, Cethegus to Quintus Cornificius," and so on with the remainder. These passages abundantly confirm what we say, to wit, that accused persons, previous to the confession of their crimes, were used to be entrusted by the Ancients to what was known as free custody, whereas after confession or conviction they were cast into the common gaol. This is corroborated by writers on Roman Law, as Venuleus, who says : "An accused person which hath confessed, pending the pronouncement of his sentence, must be cast into the public prison ; " and Scaevola, "An accused person which had confessed was, merely on the strength of his confession, used to be thrown into prison."

We would here remind the reader how Christ's faithful followers, in times of persecution, were not only shut up in the Tullianum and the Mamertine prisons, but were likewise often detained under military guard at the houses of private individuals. This is testified by innumerable Histories of the Blessed Martyrs, and in especial by those of Saints Stephen and Alexander, Roman Pontiffs.

OF CERTAIN OTHER SORTS OF BONDS.

Among these may be included *leashes* or *lashes*, employed to bind prisoners withal. Hence the name *lashers*, often mentioned in Plautus, applied to them whose duty it was to bind, or to beat, with lashes any of their fellow-slaves their master might direct. The same title was likewise given very often to the lictors and magistrates' officers who attended them when on duty in their provinces, and bore the fasces before them. —But enough said of the different sorts and kinds of bonds and of the wooden horse as used amongst the Ancients.

OF THE WOODEN HORSE, OR RACK, USED BY THE HERETICS UPON THEM OF THE ORTHODOX FAITH; OF THEIR IMPRISONMENTS, AND THE DIVERS SORTS OF TORTURES WHEREWITH THEY DO AFFLICT THE PRISONERS.

The Heretics of this present time (1591) in England (as Sanders' *Origin and Progress of the Anglican Schism,* his *Theatre of Heretic Cruelties,* and a work entitled *On the Anglican Persecution,* do testify) have tortured a number of priests, including Fathers Campion, a Religious of the Society of Jesus, Sherwin, Briant, Janson, Bosgrave, and others, to the tearing asunder of all their limbs and well-nigh to death itself, by means of an instrument called by themselves the wooden horse, or the rack. 'Tis a sort of torture wherein, after first stretching a man out on his back and binding his hands and feet joint by joint, they do little by little draw taut the ropes wherewith he is bound by certain wheels contrived to this end, till all his limbs be dislocated. This most agonising and monstrous torment is employed by these new Heretics of our day (as described in the book called *A Trophy of the English Church*) to harass withal the Catholics they have cast into prison. Beside which, they do likewise use other ways of afflicting these same prisoners, sometimes driving iron pricks and long needles under their finger-nails, sometimes (as is related of a certain priest in the work quoted just above) tying them feet uppermost to wooden posts and leaving them so a long while, till they be suffocated with the stench of their own excrements. At other times they will shut them in an instrument of iron which doth squeeze a man together and make him round like a ball, and leave them confined therein for hours together, or else drag them forcibly out of prison and hale them violently before the assemblies of heretic ministers, or binding them two and two together with chains (see again Sanders, *Anglican Schism* and *Theatre of Cruelties*), march them so from one foul and stinking dungeon to another yet more stinking and horrible. Concerning these imprisonments of Catholics in England, consult the work named above *On the Anglican Persecution*, the which I would I had space to transcribe here in full.

CHAPTER IV

Of divers Instruments employed for Scourging the Blessed Martyrs

HAVING expounded the divers sorts of bonds and thongs and the nature of the "wooden horse," we must next turn our attention to naming the various kinds of whips and scourges. For it was the frequent habit of the Heathen (as shown by sundry instances already quoted from the History of the Saints, for special ensample those of St. Crescentianus, St. Regina, virgin and martyr, and Bishop Bassus), after binding the Christians to the "horse," to beat them pitifully with rods, cudgels, whips, and the like; then to flay them with iron "claws" or similar contrivances; finally to roast them with torches, burning brands, and red-hot metal plates. Accordingly, in the first place, we propose to speak of whipping instruments; next, of iron hooks, claws, and currycombs; lastly, of torches, brands, and fiery plates.

Now as to the first named, you must know these were in use among the Ancients of many kinds, as lashes, scourges, cudgels, rods, scorpions, thongs, and loaded whips.

OF LASHES.

Plautus speaks of lashes, in the *Epidicus*, in the following terms :—

> *Ita non omnes ex cruciatu poterunt eximere Epidicum.*
> *Periphanem emere lora vidi . . .*

Also Terence, *Adelphi :*—

> *Nam si molestus pergis esse, jam intro abripiere, atque ibi*
> *Usque ad necem operiere loris.*

So too Cicero, *Philippics :*—

> *Cum eum jussu Antonii in convivio servi publici loris caeciderunt.*

("So all his friends shall not save Epidicus. I saw Periphanes buying lashes." "For if you are going to be troublesome, you shall be rushed off indoors, and there lashed to death." "When the public slaves scourged him with lashes at a feast by Antonius' orders.")

Similar mention is found again and again in the *Acts of the Martyrs*, as in the account of St. Asterius and his companions in martyrdom, of St. Euphemia, virgin and martyr, and many other witnesses of Christ of both sexes.

These lashes as used by the Ancients were thongs made of leather, employed usually (as doth follow manifestly from the passages quoted from Plautus and Terence) for the correction of slaves. So it need not surprise us in any way to find constant examples in the tales of martyrdom of Christ's faithful followers being beaten with thongs; for they were always counted by the Heathen as plebeian folk and wretches

FIG. XII.

A Martyr, bound firmly with thongs or lashes attached to his hands and feet, is violently dragged in all directions, and so torn limb from limb.

To face p. 72

of the lowest condition. These same lashes served not only (as described above) to bind the martyrs and thrash them withal, but even to tear them in pieces, as witness the *Acts of the Blessed Martyrs* concerning the passion of St. Tyrsus, where we read : "Immediately his mind (the Governor's) was filled with great wrath, and he ordered certain stalwart young men of a fierce and savage disposition to belabour the martyr with their fists. Next, after binding him with lashes attached firmly to his hands and feet, they started pulling with might and main in opposite directions, so that all the articulations of his joints were broken asunder, and he was torn limb from limb."

OF THONGS, ALSO USED FOR SCOURGING THE MARTYRS.

The word thong or nerve (as was explained in the preceding chapter) bears divers meanings. Sometimes it signifies a fastening for binding criminals withal, in which sense it hath already been treated of in that place ; but at other times a form of scourge with which the Christians, fired by love of the only true God, were beaten by the Heathen. This latter is what we have now to speak of. An animal's nerve was used for the purpose, generally a bull's. With this were beaten those most glorious athletes of Christ, Saints Ananias, Isidore, Benedicta, virgin and martyr, and many others whose names are writ in the Book of Life.

OF CUDGELS AND SCOURGES.

Cudgels and scourges were very often used for thrashing Christ's faithful followers. Scourges are spoken of by Juvenal in his *Satires*, St. Cyprian, Suetonius (*Otho*), Eusebius, and other ancient writers. They were thinner and finer than cudgels, thicker than rods. Bearing on this, we find in the Laws of Theodosius ("Of driving on the public roads, stage-drivers and couriers") the following provision : "Decreed, that no man use a cudgel for driving, but either a rod, or at most a scourge at the point whereof is set a short goad." This is sufficient to show that scourges were in use among the Ancients as above stated.

Besides Christians, persons of the humbler sort were condemned to be thrashed with these instruments, as Plautus, *Amphitryon*, doth imply, and even the Vestal Virgins themselves, if by their neglect the fire impiously consecrated to Vesta, the Romans' false goddess, had been suffered to go out. See Valerius Maximus and Livy the Historian. However, to return to the Blessed Martyrs of our Lord Jesus Christ, we find that very many of these were beaten with scourges and cudgels—with cudgels, Saints Felix and Alexander, Privatus and Bassus, Bishops, Julius, a Senator, and many others ; with scourges, the Blessed Martyrs Neophytus, Julianus, Tryphon, Sabbatius, and countless others, whose names are forgotten. Of these we find this record in the *Roman Martyrology* under February 20 : "Commemoration of the Blessed Martyrs at Tyre in Phœnicia, the number whereof is known only to God. Under the Emperor Diocletian and by order of Veturius, master of the soldiers, these were slain with many kinds of torments following one after the other. First, were their whole bodies torn with scourges ;

then were they delivered to various kinds of wild beasts, but by divine goodness in no wise hurt by them; finally given up cruelly to fire and sword, they so won the crown of martyrdom."

I must here tell you that the Christians were sometimes beaten so long with cudgels and scourges that they died under the lash. Thus perished those gallant soldiers of Christ, Saints Sebastian; Julius, a Senator; Maxima, virgin and martyr; Eusebius, Sabbatius, and many more of either sex.

OF CUDGELLING, DECIMATION, AND OTHER MILITARY PUNISHMENTS.

Seeing we often read in the Histories of the Saints how Christians, and especially Christian soldiers, were by way of ignominy condemned to dig, beaten with cudgels and rods, stripped of the military belt, and decimated, all and sundry of which were forms of punishment for Roman soldiers guilty of various offences, we have therefore resolved to specify here of what sort and number these penalties were. They were numerous, some less and some more severe. For whereas within the City walls the Portian Law safeguarded Roman citizens against the Magistrates' rods and axes, this was not the case in camps and in the field. For the Laws drew a distinction betwixt military discipline and civil, and betwixt the terror needful to bend an army to obedience and that required to govern a peaceful people. For from the orders of a General in the field there was no appeal.

Lighter penalties inflicted on soldiers were such as involved disgrace and degradation only, as to be dismissed the service with ignominy, to be mulcted of their proper pay, to give up their spear, to change their quarters, to winter in the open country, to eat their rations standing, to dig a trench, to be unbelted and disarmed, to be fed on barley, to be blooded by opening a vein.

Graver punishments were such as caused bodily harm, as to be beaten with rods, to be sold into slavery, to be struck with a cudgel or an axe, to be decimated, to be crucified. Of all these we shall find well-authenticated and notorious instances in Sigonius, book i., *On the Ancient Civil Law of the Romans.*

And first as to dismissal from the service with ignominy, this is mentioned and described in Aulus Hirtius in the following terms: "Cæsar, speaking from the *suggestus* (platform) and addressing the assembled Tribunes and Centurions of all the Legions, said thus, Whereas, Caius Avienus, in Italy you have stirred up Roman soldiers against the Commonwealth, and have plundered the provincial towns, I hereby expel you with ignominy from my army."

As to deprivation of pay, this is well enough understood, I take it, already. I may add that the phrase "broken in pay" was applied (so Nonius states) to those soldiers whose pay, in order to brand them with disgrace, was stopped, that is to say, the sum of money representing their gains for a month, or a year, was confiscated. So Varro, quoted by the same author, speaking of the life and habits of the Roman people, writes: "What was known as a soldier's pay was the money given him half-yearly or yearly; when his pay was stopped as a mark of disgrace, he was said to be *broken of his pay*." Livy again says: "As a mark of disgrace, it was decreed this legion should receive a half-year's pay in lieu of a whole year's."

Now with regard to other punishments, as that of surrendering the spear, Festus explains the matter thus: "Penalty of the spear so called was when a soldier was sentenced by way of punishment for a military offence to hand in his spears."

As to changing quarters in camp, Polybius tells us that if it was wished to stigmatise soldiers with disgrace, these were ordered to pitch outside the camp. Accordingly in Livy, we find the men who had been beaten at Cannæ complaining: "Now are we reduced to a worse condition than returned prisoners of war had to suffer in former days. For only their arms, and their position in the line and the place where they might pitch in camp were changed, all which they could recover by one good achievement for their country's good or one successful battle."

As to winter quarters, read Livy (book xxvi.): "A further disgrace was inflicted in every case, viz. that they should not winter in a town, nor construct winter quarters within a distance of ten miles of any city." As to rations, the same author (book xxiv.) writes: "The names of all who, thinking of their previous defeat, lately withdrew from their post, I shall order to be reported to me, and summoning each before me, shall bind one and all on oath never, except in case of sickness, to take food or drink otherwise than standing, so long as they shall remain in the service."

As to digging, we may appeal to Plutarch, who says in his *Lucullus* that it was an old form of military disgrace for culprits to be compelled to strip to their shirts and dig a trench, while the rest of the troops looked on."

As to other penalties mentioned, see Livy again (book xxvii.) : "The cohorts which had lost their standards, he ordered to be served with barley ; and the Centurions of those maniples whose standards had been lost, he unbelted and deprived of their swords." Polybius also speaks of barley being served out instead of wheat as a mark of disgrace.

As to letting blood as a punishment, Aulus Gellius hath the following, "This was another old-fashioned military punishment, to order by way of ignominy a vein to be opened and the offender blooded."

Concerning other and more severe forms of punishment the passages next quoted will serve as evidence. Livy writing of Scipio's reform of military discipline before Numantia, "Any soldier he caught out of the ranks, he scourged—if he were a Roman citizen, with staves, if a foreigner, with cudgels," and in another place, " Publius Nasica and Decius Brutus, the two Consuls, held a review of the troops, on which occasion a punishment was inflicted likely to have an excellent effect on the minds of the recruits, before whom it was carried out. A certain Caius Matienus, who had been accused before the Tribunes of the People of desertion from the army in Spain and condemned to the *fork*, or pillory, was beaten with rods

for a long while, and then sold into slavery for a sesterce."[1]
Also Cicero, *Philippics*, "The legions deserved *cudgelling*
which deserted the Consul, if he was Consul."

Now, according to Polybius, this punishment of cudgelling
was inflicted in this fashion. First the Tribune took up a
cudgel and just touched the condemned man with it; after
which, all who were in camp at the time set to, beating the
culprit with cudgels and pelting him with stones, and generally
killed him inside the camp. Nay, if any did escape, they
were no better off, seeing they could neither return to their
fatherland, nor be harboured at home by their relations.

The most ancient instance of decimation is recorded by
Livy as carried out in his Consulship by Appius Claudius, a
man of a very stern and harsh disposition. To quote the
Historian's words, "Appius Claudius the Consul called a
general muster and rebuked the troops as disloyal to military
discipline and deserters from the colours,—and not without
good reason. Turning to individual soldiers whom he saw
unarmed, he demanded where their standards and their
weapons were, asking a similar question of ensigns who had
lost their colours, as well as Centurions and double-pay men
who had forsaken the ranks, and finally had them beaten to
death with rods. Of the remaining rank and file, each tenth
man was chosen out by lot for punishment." The mode of
carrying out such an order is detailed by the same author, who
writes concerning Scipio's punishing of his mutinous army at
Suero, "Then was heard the voice of the herald proclaiming

[1] *Sestertius,* a small silver coin—value, twopence and a fraction.

the names of those condemned in the council. These were now stripped and dragged forward, while at the same moment all the paraphernalia of punishment were exhibited ; then they were lashed to a stake and beaten with rods or felled with an axe."

Crucifixion as a military punishment is likewise mentioned by Livy: "Deserters to the enemy were more severely dealt with than mere runaways. Such as were of the Latin Name were beheaded, while Roman offenders were crucified."

Such then were the divers sorts of military punishments. That these did continue in use down to the very end of the Republican period, Suetonius is evidence sufficient, when he says of Augustus, "Any cohorts which had given ground, he decimated and fed the survivors on barley ; Centurions who had deserted their post and likewise Manipulars in the same case he punished with death. For other offences he inflicted divers ignominious penalties—such as to stand all day in front of the Prætorium, or headquarters, in some instances wearing the tunic only and stripped of their belts, others holding a ten-foot pole or even carrying a sod of earth."

So much for military punishments. Now as regards Christian soldiers which won the Crown of Martyrdom at the hands of the Heathen, it is to be noted (as recorded in their several *Histories*) how these were sometimes condemned to dig the ground or else were decimated, sometimes and very frequently beaten with cudgels and rods, or stripped,—that is deprived of the military belt.

As to Christian soldiers being condemned to dig the

FIG. XIII.

Martyrs tied to a post set upright in the ground, to a stake or pillar, and persistently beaten
with cudgels till they died.

To face p. 80

ground, testimony is afforded by the History of St. Marcellus, Pope, wherein is writ concerning them, "At the date when Maximianus returned from the parts of Africa to the City of Rome, being wishful to please Diocletian, and further his design of building Thermæ, or Baths, to be called after his name, he began, out of hatred towards the Christians, to constrain all soldiers of that Faith, whether Romans or foreigners, to forced labour, and in divers places to condemn the same, some to quarrying stone, other to digging sand." The same may also be found recorded in the *Acts* of St. Severa, a Roman Virgin.

Decimation again is attested by the Histories of those most Blessed Martyrs of Christ, St. Maurice and his companions, where it is writ, "Let the fatal lot give every tenth man to death,"—and what else was decimation but so putting to death every tenth soldier? Read further on this, an if you will, the Roman Historian Tacitus, "Every tenth man of the disgraced cohort was chosen by lot and cudgelled to death," and again, "Forasmuch as every tenth man of the beaten army is beaten to death, even brave men are at times chosen out by the lot."

The next punishment, cudgelling to wit, doth make a part of the passion of nearly all those martyred Christian soldiers which did find it a pleasant and a joyful thing to be rid of this poor, brief life for Christ's sake.

One thing we would have the reader note, namely that not alone Christian soldiers were belaboured with cudgels, but other faithful servants of Christ in like wise; for the Laws of the Romans did duly decree that whosoever should profess themselves filled with God's grace should be beaten with cudgels for their penalty.

Finally, other testimonies to the same fact are to be read in the *Acts* of St. Hesychius, of St. Marcellus a Centurion, of Saints Eudoxius, Zeno, Macarius, and their companions, one hundred and four in number, and many others. In especial do we learn from the *Acts* of the aforesaid St. Marcellus how that the military belt, so often mentioned, was nothing more nor less than the ordinary soldier's sword-belt, or rather baldrick, for we find writ therein, "In the city of Tingitana, when Fortunatus was Procurator and Commander of the Troops, the Emperor's birthday came round. So when all were indulging in merrymakings and offering sacrifices, one Marcellus, a Centurion of the Legion of Trajan, deeming the said rejoicings to be profane, threw off his military belt before the standards of the legion which were there and then present, and testified with a loud voice, saying, "I am a soldier of Jesus Christ, the King everlasting." Likewise he cast away his Centurion's staff and his arms, further declaring, "From this day forth I make an end of fighting for your Emperors. . . ." But the soldiers, astounded to hear such words, did seize him and report the matter to Astasianus Fortunatus, Commander of the Legion, which did order him to be put in prison. Presently when the feasting was ended, he took his seat at the council board and ordered Marcellus the Centurion to be brought in ; this being done, Astasianus Fortunatus, the Commander, thus addressed him : "What hath been your intent that, in defiance of military discipline, you did ungird your belt and throw away your baldrick and staff?" Then some lines lower down, "This soldier, casting off his military belt, hath openly proclaimed himself to be a Christian, and publicly before all the folk hath spoken many blasphemies against the gods and against Cæsar. Wherefore have we referred this thing to you, that whatsoever your wisdom shall see fit to direct, may be duly carried out." Such the words addressed by his gaolers concerning the Blessed Marcellus to Agricolaus the Judge, to whom he had sub-sequently been sent to be tried. Now when we read at the beginning of this account how Marcellus cast away his military belt; and again lower down, how being charged before the Commander, he did cast away his baldrick; and yet again, when the soldiers were stating the case against him before Agricolaus, his belt once more,—it is abundantly plain these were one and the same thing. In fact a baldrick, if we may believe the authority of Varro, *On the Latin Tongue*, was a belt of leather decorated with studs or bosses and worn aslant from the right shoulder to the left hip. So Quintilian writes, "That fold which is carried aslant from right shoulder across to the left side, like a baldrick, must be neither too chokingly tight nor yet too loose."

One point here we would have the reader to observe, to wit how the constancy of Christian soldiers was such, and such their burning desire to suffer for Christ's sake, that it is a very frequent thing to find mention of their having, voluntarily and in contempt and defiance of the heathen emperors and other great officers, cast off the military belt. Thus we read of St. Hesychius: "Now he was a soldier, and having heard read the order of Maximianus to the effect that any which should refuse to make sacrifice to idols, should lay off his military belt, suddenly and of his own motion he did unbuckle his own;" and again of St. Eudoxius and his sainted companions: "Eudoxius did instantly remove his girdle and toss it in the Commander's face. This act seeming to his comrades a direct appeal and call to emulation, the whole number of them that stood around, an hundred and four in all, did likewise hurl their belts in his face."—So much for the pains and penalties inflicted on Christian soldiers.

OF RODS, AND SCORPIONS.

Frequent mention is made of rods wherewith prisoners were beaten in divers plays of Plautus, by Valerius Maximus, by Cicero, as well as by Prudentius in the Hymn of St. Romanus.

Rods among the Ancients were of many sorts,—some of elm-wood, as Plautus saith in the *Asinaria :*—

Ipsos, qui tibi subvectabant rure huc virgas ulmeas, . . .

and a little further on in the same play :—

Mihi tibique interminatus 'st, nos futuros ulmeos.

("The very fellows that used to bring you your supply of elm-rods from the country." "He threatened you and me, we should presently feel the elm.")

Thus Plautus,—showing us the Ancients were in the

constant habit of correcting their slaves with these rods of elm-wood.

Others again were made of birch, of which tree Pliny hath left a description in these words : "This Gallic tree (the birch, to wit) is of a remarkable glossiness and slenderness, a terrible material for the rods used by magistrates. Its flexibility makes it equally convenient for hoops as well as for the plaited work of baskets."

Yet others again were of oak, others of ash, others of willow. Rods of the first sort are named in the *Acts* of St. Acatius, a Centurion, of the third by Prudentius in his Hymn of St. Romanus in these lines :—

> *Cum puer torqueretur jussu Praesidis,*
> *Impacta quoties corpus attigerat salix,*
> *Tenui rubebant sanguine uda vimina.*

("Whenas the lad was tortured by the Governor's orders, every time the willow struck and wealed his body, the switches grew wet and red with drops of blood"); in confirmation whereof we may further quote from the *Epidicus* of Plautus :—

> *Lictores duo, duo viminei fasces virgarum*

("Two apparitors and two bundles of willow rods and switches "). Switches, in fact, are made of poplar twigs, of elm, red wood, birch, vine, twisted hazel, or willow, which last is best for the purpose.

OF RODS MADE OF VINE WOOD.

Rods made of vine wood were used for beating military offenders, in which connection we should not fail to observe how that the Centurions' sign of office was a vine staff, wherewith they were wont to chastise soldiers over slow in obeying. This is shown in Pliny: "The vine staff in the Centurion's hand is an excellent specific for bringing sluggish troops to the colours, and when used to chastise offences makes even the punishment respectable;" and Tacitus: "The Centurion Lucillus is killed in a mutiny,—an officer nicknamed in soldiers' slang 'Give us another,' because after breaking his staff over a soldier's back, he would loudly call for another, and then another." So too Juvenal writing of Caius Marius in his *Eighth Satire :—*

> *Nodosam post haec frangebat vertice vitem,*
> *Si lentus pigra munires castra dolabra.*

("Then he would strike you o' the head with a knotty staff, if you were over slow in entrenching and sluggish in your spade work.")—But enough said of rods made of vine wood.

OF RODS OF IRON AND LEAD.

Albeit rods for beating offenders withal were generally made of thin twigs of trees, yet sometimes were they of iron or lead. This is shown in divers *Acts* of the Blessed Martyrs, as those of Saints Paul and Juliana, Saints Christopher and Callinicus, and others.

OF PRICKLY RODS, OTHERWISE CALLED SCORPIONS.

Not alone with smooth rods were the Ancients used to chastise offenders, and Christians amongst the rest, but likewise with knotty and prickly ones, which they appropriately named "scorpions." And so whenever we find it recorded in accounts of the marytrdom of the saints, how that such and such faithful servants of Christ were beaten with thorny, prickly, and knotty rods, 'tis the same thing as though it were writ that they had been scourged with *scorpions*.

Rods, then, as explained above, were either smooth or prickly. If the first sort, they were either of twigs or of metal. If of twigs, either of elm, birch, oak, ash, or lastly willow; but if of metal, either of iron, and this sometimes red-hot, or of lead. Further may be appended what is said of rods in the *Histories* of Saints Hermillus and Stratonicus, to this effect: "Greatly angered at these words, Licinus orders Stratonicus to be stretched face upward and thrashed on the belly with rods of a three-cornered shape. Now this was a grievous torture, scarce tolerable by the human frame, forasmuch as the corners of the rods cruelly cut the flesh like so many swords."

Moreover, it should be understood that not only were the martyrs named above, Saints Acatius, Paul, Christopher, Callinicus, Hermillus, and Stratonicus, beaten with smooth rods, but many others likewise, to wit, Saints Pontianus, Zeno, Theodore, Paula a virgin, Regina, Claudius, and an host of others of either sex. But with knotty and prickly rods, or *scorpions*, those glorious soldiers of Christ, Saints Basil, Cyrinus, Bassus a Bishop, Symphorian, Nicostratus, Simplicius, and countless others.

We should further note that, albeit beating with rods was a form of punishment held ignominious among the Ancients, yet was it, notwithstanding this fact, a lighter penalty than certain others. The ignominy attaching thereto is shown by sundry laws of the Romans, the Porcian Law, the Symphronian, etc., as well as from direct statement of the ancient authorities. Read Cicero for instance, *Pro Rabirio*, and the same Orator's speeches against Verres; likewise Josephus' *Jewish War*, where it is spoke of as something extraordinary that Caestius Florus did scourge Jews enjoying Roman citizenship with rods, and fasten them in the criminals' collar or pillory.

Last, but not least, I would have it known how the Catholics are often beaten with rods by the heretics of our own time (1591). This is shown by Sanders, *The Anglican Schism*, who says: "Nor should this be left unmentioned, that sundry of the common folk, for refusing to attend the churches and profane services of the Protestants, and seeing they had not money wherewith to pay a fine, were by the judge's orders long and cruelly dragged through the city of Winchester, stripped naked, and savagely beaten with rods." The fashion wherein this is done is declared in the *Theatre of Cruelties* in these words: "The Catholics were tied at the cart's tail, and so whipped through the streets."

FIG. XIV.

A. Martyr bound to four stakes and beaten with cudgels.
B. Martyr laid naked on iron spikes and violently beaten with a cudgel.

C. Martyr bound hand and foot and similarly beaten with a cudgel.

To face p. 88

Of Divers Instruments employed for Scourging

OF LOADED SCOURGES, WHEREWITH THE MARTYRS WERE BEATEN.

Loaded scourges (as the *Histories* of the Blessed Martyrs do indicate, and Prudentius to boot, and certain paintings to be viewed here in Rome) were a sort of whipping instrument made of cords or thongs, to the ends whereof little balls of lead were fastened, and with which the loins, back, and neck of a condemned person were thrashed. This sort of scourge is mentioned in the accounts of very many martyrdoms, as well as by Prudentius, who writes thus in his Hymn of St. Romanus :—

> *Tundatus tergum crebris ictibus,*
> *Plumboque cervix verberata extuberet :*
> *Persona quaeque competenter plectitur,*
> *Magnique refert, vilis sit, an nobilis.*

("Let his back be pounded with quick-falling blows, and his neck scourged with lead till it swell up : each is appropriately punished, and it makes no small difference whether he be a common fellow or a noble.")

In fact it was customary with the Ancients to punish only persons of the commoner sort with loaded scourges. The same sort of punishment was still in vogue in the days of the Emperor Honorius, who beat that impious heresiarch Jovinian and his vile associates with loaded whips, before finally banishing them into exile.

Now albeit scourging with these loaded whips was not meant to kill criminals, and it was actually forbid by an enactment of the civil law to beat a prisoner to death, yet many are found to have breathed their last under the blows of these cruel instruments. This is implied by Ammianus Marcellinus, and in an *Epistle* of Ambrosius, wherein he writes : "What answer shall I make afterward, if it be discovered that, on authority from me, Christians have been killed, whether with the sword, with cudgels, or with loaded whips?" Now Christians which did so lay down their lives for Christ were : Sts. Maximus, Papias, Severa a Roman virgin, with her brothers Marcus and Calendius, also Sts. Gervasius, Januarius, Concordia, Privatus, Severus, Severianus, and countless others, whose names we must pass over for the sake of brevity. Further, we read of sundry other faithful servants of Christ which were beaten with loaded scourges, but without losing their lives under this treatment. Such were (to name a few only) Saints Laurence, Artemius, Procopius, Gordian, Erasmus and Theodore Bishops.

OF OTHER WAYS WHEREIN LEAD WAS USED IN THE TORTURING OF THE HOLY MARTYRS.

Lead was likewise employed by the Ancients for torturing prisoners in two other fashions. First, after stripping them stark naked, they would pour it in a boiling state over their bodies,—a form of punishment we shall speak of more at length in Chapter IX. below. Secondly, they made use of it on occasion neither for scourging nor burning with, but for straining and dislocating the several joints of persons condemned to this torture, whose arms being twisted backward and fastened above their heads, leaden weights were then hung to their feet. Such leaden weights are referred to by Ammianus, when he says, "Then are the leaden weights got ready." If the reader would learn more concerning them, let him read the *Histories* of the Blessed Martyrs, St. Justus and St. Mamans.

OF THE FASHION WHEREIN PRISONERS WERE BEATEN BY THE ANCIENTS.

The custom of the Ancients was, when prisoners were to be scourged, first to strip the same, and then to whip them over the back, or belly, or other portion of the body, with rods or other instruments of flagellation. And this the apparitors did carry out in many divers ways. Sometimes they would tie them up to stakes set upright in the ground or to pillars; sometimes they would stretch them on the earth or else over sharp spikes a foot high fixed in the ground; at others suspending their victims aloft with bodies hanging straight down, or else mounting them on another's shoulders as boys do, and lashing their posteriors. Yet another way was to fix four pegs in the ground, forcibly stretch them out and bind them hand and foot to these, then after kindling a fire underneath to their still bitterer torment, to thrash them unmercifully. Moreover the magistrates of the Roman people were always used to command their apparitors, or lictors as they were called, first to strip and lay naked their victims which were to be punished, as is clearly shown by the most of the *Acts* of the Holy Martyrs, especially those of Saints Ananias, Secundianus, Clement of Ancyra, St. Barbara Virgin and Martyr, St. Apollinaris Bishop, and others.

Further corroboration and more certain evidence of this may be gathered from many writings of the Ancients themselves, whereby it will likewise be established how that the judges and magistrates of the Roman people were used by way of punishing a criminal to order their officers to strip and lay naked the same, as aforesaid, and then employ their rods and axes upon him. Thus Livy writes, "The Consuls command the man to be stripped, and the axes made ready. 'I appeal,' cries Volero, 'to the People; seeing how the Tribunes had rather see a Roman citizen beaten with rods before their eyes than themselves murdered in their beds by you.' But the more furiously he shouted, the more fierce was the lictor in tearing off his clothes and stripping him naked." And the same Historian in another place, speaking of Papirius Cursor, "He bade the lictor make ready his axe. At this command the Prænestine stood astounded, but the other only said, 'Now to it, lictor, and cut away yonder stump, which is a hindrance to the traffic.'" Also Valerius Maximus, relating the same story, says, "He commanded the rods to be got ready and the man to be stripped," and Livy once more, in another book of his History, "Then Papirius was roused to fresh anger and ordered the Master of the Horse to be stripped naked, and the rods and axes to be got ready." So likewise Cicero, in his speech *In Verrem*, saith, "Accordingly he commands the man to be seized and stripped naked in the open forum and bound, and the rods to be made ready." All these passages then do plainly prove that prisoners were beaten by the lictors only after being first stripped of their clothing.

Of Divers Instruments employed for Scourging

Now the fact that the Blessed Martyrs were whipped with lashes on the back or belly or both or any other portion of the body is plainly shown in the *Acts* of the Martyrs, Saints Clement of Ancyra and Ananias, above named, as well as of St. Claudius and his companions. That they were beaten in old days by the Heathen, after being tied up by the lictors to stakes or pillars, stretched out on the ground or over sharp spikes fixed in the earth, or else strongly bound to four pegs, as above described, may be proved from many passages, to wit from many and many *Acts* of the Blessed Martyrs, as those of Saints Paul and Juliana, Eulampius and Eulampia, brother and sister, Saint Anastasia, a Roman virgin and martyr, and an host of others. Read again in this connection what we have laid down in Chapter I. above concerning stakes, pillars and trees, whereto Christians were suspended to be tortured.

Lastly that the Holy Martyrs were beaten as boys are thrashed may be learned from Prudentius' Hymn of St. Romanus, where Asclepiades gives orders concerning a boy Barula, whom all unwillingly and unwittingly he was about to consecrate a Blessed Martyr to Christ :—

> . . . *pusionem praecipit*
> *Sublime tollant, et manu pulsent nates.*
> *Mox et remota veste, virgis verberent,*
> *Tenerumque duris ictibus tergum secent,*
> *Plus unde lactis quam cruoris defluat.*

(" . . . He bids them lift the lad aloft and beat his buttocks with their hands ; then anon stripping off his clothes, thrash him with rods, and rend his tender loins with heavy blows,—wherefrom more milk may well flow than blood.")

But it was not only boys, like Vitus and Barula, that were thrashed in boy fashion as being mere lads, but others likewise of riper age and of either sex,—a practice followed, it would appear, in order to involve greater ignominy and disgrace. Thus was St. Thomas, a most reverend Bishop, beaten,—as we find writ in Victor, *On the Vandal War*,—as also St. Afra.

OF THE OFFICERS WHOSE DUTY IT WAS IN ANCIENT TIMES TO BEAT PRISONERS.

The officers which were used to beat prisoners by order of the Magistrates were called Lictors. These appertained to Consuls, Proconsuls, and the like, Consul and Proconsul having twelve each, other magistrates six, with the sole exception of the City Prætor, who had only two. The lictors walked before each magistrate, bearing bundles of rods tied up with an axe in the midst, and known as *fasces*, so that whenever ordered, they might unfasten the same, and first thrashing the condemned man with their rods, afterwards strike him down with the axe. These facts may be readily confirmed from many witnesses among Ancient writers. To take Cicero first, who saith in his great speech *Against Verres:* "Six stalwart lictors stand round him, men well practised in beating and thrashing criminals;" then Livy, "Go, lictor, bind him to the stake." The same, too, is proven by the mournful formula, wherewith the lictor was commanded to inflict the customary penalty on a traitor. This was, "Go, lictor, bind his hands; cover his head; hang him to the accursed tree." Thus Livy writes of the Publius Horatius concerned in the matter of the Horatii and Curiatii : "So the Duumviri condemned him to death; then one of them addressing Publius Horatius, saith, 'I do pronounce thee, Publius Horatius, guilty of high treason. Go, lictor, bind his hands';" and a little further on again, " 'This same man,' he went on, 'whom you saw but now, Quirites, walking honoured, triumphant and victorious, can you bear to behold standing beneath the gallows, bound and enduring lashes and torments?' And when the eyes of the Albans could scarce endure so hideous a spectacle, 'Go, lictor,' he cried, 'bind his hands,—those hands which so lately were armed and winning empire for the Roman People. Go, cover the head of the liberator of this city; hang him to the accursed tree; scourge him, either within the bounds, that is amid yonder spears and spoils of the foe, or else without, that is amid the tombs of the Curiatii.'"

To complete our account, we may append further what Aulus Gellius hath left on record concerning lictors : "Moreover the lictors had other duties to perform ; it was their office not only to bind and beat criminals and strike them with their axe, but also to hang them, if need were ; whence the words, 'Go, lictor, bind his hands, cover his head, hang him to the accursed tree.'" Beside all which, it belonged to the same officers to clear folk out of the road, on occasion to silence such as spake over lengthily, and even to strangle criminals, as Plutarch demonstrates in his *Life of Cicero*, writing thus of Lentulus : "First the Consul removes Lentulus from the Palatium, and marches him along the Sacred Way and through the midst of the Forum. Then on leaving the Forum and arriving at the gaol, he hands his prisoner over to the lictor, and ordered him to be strangled." Yet another duty of the lictors was to visit the houses of persons wanted in Court and to strike on the doors with a rod, for to summon them thither. —But enough of lictors and their offices.

OF DIVERS OTHER FASHIONS WHEREIN THE MARTYRS WERE USED TO BE STRUCK AND BEATEN BY THE HEATHEN.

Blows, buffets, and boxes o' the ear were likewise lavished ofttimes on the Blessed Christian Martyrs, and kicks and fisticuffs ; while their faces were bruised with stones and their jaws broken, or themselves overwhelmed under the same and so done to death. Blows, buffets, and kicks were the fate of those most glorious heralds of our Faith, Saints Marcellinus a priest, Epipodius, Aquilina, Tatiana, Felicitas, Speusippus, Eleusippus, Meleusippus, and lastly Pothenus, or Pothinus, Bishop of Lyons, whose death Eusebius in his *Ecclesiastical History* thus describes : "Likewise the Sainted Pothenus, to whom the Bishopric of Lugdunum (Lyons) had been entrusted. He had now overpassed the ninetieth year of his age, and was so sore exhausted with bodily weakness he could scarce draw breath freely by reason of his extreme infirmity ; yet was his spirit greatly refreshed and his mind grown alert by the burning desire he had of martyrdom. So he advanced boldly to the tribunal, and albeit his body was well-nigh worn out by the decrepitude of advanced age and the tortures of disease, yet was his soul preserved intact within him to triumph gloriously in its steadfastness for Christ. Led by the

FIG. XV.

A. Martyr buffeted, kicked, and pounded with the fists.
B. Martyr being stoned.

C. Martyr whose face and jaws are bruised and broken with a stone.
D. Martyr crushed under a huge stone

96a

To face p. 96

soldiers to the bar, the magistrates of the city going with him, and the whole multitude of the people shouting insults at him as a Christian, he did exhibit a noble testimony to the Faith. For whereas he was asked by the Presiding Judge, who was the God of the Christians? he made answer, 'If thou be worthy to know this thing, thou shalt know it.' Wherefore was he roughly and piteously dragged thence, and received many blows, both from them which were standing near by, who nothing respecting his years, did cuff and kick him shamefully and insultingly, and likewise from others further away, who threw at him whatsoever each had in his hand. This they did, forasmuch as each and all deemed it a great fault and an act of impiety, if any man failed wherever he stood to do some insolence to his person, holding that by so doing they were serving the cause of their false gods. Finally, he was cast, scarce breathing, into the common gaol, where two days later he gave up the ghost." Thus Eusebius writes concerning the death of St. Pothenus. A like end was that of the Blessed Martyr, St. Fabius.

OF BLOWS, BUFFETS, AND SLAPS.

These three words are held by some to be synonymous, but that this is not so is plainly shown by many tokens. Thus St. Matthew, ch. xxvi.: "Then did they spit in His face and buffet Him : and some smote Him with the palms of their hands;" St. Mark, ch. xiv. : "And some began to spit on Him, and to cover His face, and to buffet Him . . . and the officers received Him with blows of their hands;" St. John, ch. xviii. : ". . . one of the officers standing by struck Jesus with his hand."

From these passages it is plainly evident that the word *buffet* must be understood of a slap struck with the palm or open hand, while a *blow* is one inflicted with the clenched fist. This is further confirmed by Martial (Epigrams) :—

O quam dignus eras alapis, Mariane, Latini!

("Oh! how well deserving wast thou, Marianus, of Latinus' slaps!"); and Terence, *Adelphi :—*

Ne mora sit, si innuerim, quin pugnus continuo in mala haereat

("Not a moment's delay, when I give the sign; but batter his face instantly with your fist"); and a little further on in the same play :—

Homini misero plus quingentos colaphos infregit mihi

("Wretch that I am, he struck me above five hundred blows with his fist"); and again :—

Omnes dentes labefecit mihi;
Praeterea colaphis tuber est totum caput.

("He loosened all my teeth; besides which my head is all one swelling from his fisticuffs.")

This distinction between fist and palm, fisticuff and slap, is well illustrated by a remark Cicero makes in his treatise entitled *The Orator :* "Doubling up his fingers and making a fist, Zeno was used to say, 'That's what Dialectic is like;' then loosening his grip and opening his hand, he would add, 'But Eloquence resembles this open hand.'" He said, in fact, the Rhetorician or Orator was like the open hand; the

Dialectician like the fist, because while the former spake at greater length, the latter argued in a more compressed and forcible fashion. Fisticuffs, then, or blows are dealt with the clenched fist, buffets or slaps with the open palm. But an if the reader would gain further information concerning this form of penalty and ignominy, wherewith women in especial were punished for the Christian faith, let him read what Aulus Gellius hath to say on the subject.

OF MARTYRS WHICH HAD THEIR FACES BEAT IN WITH STONES, FEATURES BRUISED, OR THEIR JAWS BROKEN.

Christians which were subjected to the above-named modes of martyrdom are Saints Papias, Maurus, Theodosia, Felix a priest, Apollinaris a Bishop, Felicissima virgin and martyr, beside the forty soldiers which be mentioned in the *Roman Martyrology* under March 9: "At Sebasté in Armenia, anniversary of the forty sainted Cappadocian soldiers, which in the days of Licinius and under the Governorship of Agricolaus, after enduring bonds and most cruel imprisonment, and after their faces had been beat with stones, were thrown into a frozen pond, where their bodies, stiffened by the frost, were broken in sunder, and they did consummate their martyrdom by the fracture of their limbs. And of these two were of noble birth, Cyrion and Candidus by name. The pre-eminent glory of them all hath been renowned in the writings of St. Basil and of others."

Polybius, too, dealing with military punishments, doth relate how in Ancient times soldiers were not only beaten with cudgels, but likewise stoned; but of their punishments generally we have already treated in our remarks upon cudgels and cudgellings.

OF MARTYRS WHICH WERE STONED, AND SO GAVE UP THEIR LIVES TO DEATH.

Amongst Saints which were stoned to death are numbered such most renowned martrys as St. Stephen the Proto-martyr, St. Demetrius and his companions, Saints Cyriacus, Tranquillinus, Diocletius, beside the most glorious Emerentiana and Paula, virgins and martyrs.

OF GREAT STONES WHEREWITH THE CHRISTIANS WERE PRESSED AND VERY GRIEVOUSLY TORMENTED.

Moreover, by means of great stones and rocks were the Christian servants of Our Lord tortured in divers ways. Sometimes we read of their being crushed under great boulders; thus in the *Acts* of the Blessed Martyr St. Theopompus it is writ, "Hereupon the holy man was led forth ·from his prison and stretched face upward on the ground and bound fast to stakes; then was a huge boulder, that eight men could scarce carry, laid upon his belly. But the great stone was lifted up from off him by the divine efficacy. . . ." Again in the *Acts* of the Martyr St. Victor is found, "Being brought out of prison after three days, he did kick over with his foot a statue of Jupiter which was presented to him, to the end he might offer incense thereto. The offending foot is instantly cut off, and the holy man laid under a millstone, wherewith he is cruelly ground. But lo! after a little the mill brake in pieces of itself, while yet the Martyr of the Lord was breathing faintly." Again in the *Acts* of the most Blessed Martyr, St. Artemius, this account is to be read, "Hearing these words and being filled with wrath, Julian called stonemasons to him and said, 'See you yonder block of stone?'—pointing to one that had broke from the front of the Amphitheatre. 'Divide me it into two halves. Then, laying the one half flat on the earth, stretch out this male-factor upon the same, and let down the other half heavily upon him, so that caught betwixt the two he may have both flesh and bones crushed out of all shape. By this means he shall learn whom he is trying to resist and what help he may expect from his God.' No sooner said than done, and the holy man being imprisoned betwixt the two stones, so great was the weight pressing upon his body that as his bones brake asunder, a sound of splitting and cracking was actually heard of many. For all his inwards were torn to pieces and the articulations of his bones crushed, while his eyes started out of their sockets. Yet albeit he was reduced to such sore straits, did he not neglect to sing to God's praise; for he chanted where he lay betwixt the stone, saying, 'Thou hast exalted and brought me up, for Thou art my hope, and a tower of strength in the face of mine enemy; Thou hast set my feet on a rock and guided my steps aright. Receive therefore my spirit, Thou only beloved Son of God, and deliver me not up into the hands of my foes!' So finally, when he had now remained a day and a night inside the stones, the wicked

Julian commanded the two blocks to be separated, thinking that he had surely perished betwixt them and that no vestige of life was yet left him under so grievous and overwhelming a weight. But lo! no sooner was he freed of the stones, than he came forth walking on his own feet,—verily a miracle worthy of all wonder and admiration! A man, naked and unprotected, whose eyes had started out of his head, whose bones had been crushed and all his limbs and flesh squeezed into one mass by the weight of the stone, so that his bowels had miserably gushed out, this man—oh, strange and unexampled sight!—was walking and talking, and speaking words of rebuke against the tyrant, so that even he was astounded. . . ." Another relation of a like martyrdom by means of great stones is found in the *History* of St. Joseph in the following words, "Then after removing the holy man to some little distance and binding his hands behind him, they dig a pit for him and bury him therein up to the middle. Then they set round about him the Christians they had arrested, and order these to pelt and assail the noble victim with stones. But when amongst the rest they urged the blessed and holy Isdandul to do likewise, she said, ' Never before in the world's history was heard such a thing, that a woman be compelled to lift her hand against holy men, as now you would have me do. 'Tis not against your enemies you are fighting, but against us your friends are you taking arms, and filling with blood and carnage your native land, which was in peace and quietness.' Then they did fasten a spike to the end of a long reed and bade her prick the holy man with the same. But she cried,

'Far be it from me to do this thing. Rather would I drive it through mine own heart than inflict the smallest scratch on his sainted body.' Thus did she manifest a manly constancy, and showed her stronger than those murderers had deemed possible.

"But now did they overwhelm the saint with such a snow-storm of stones that his head alone remained visible, all the rest of him being buried beneath a heap of stones. And when one of the ruffians saw the head still moving, he orders one of the lictors to take a stone as big as he could wield and throw it down on him. So when this was done and his head crushed by the weight of the stone, the saint thus gave up his precious soul to Christ." So much for what the *Acts* of the Saints have to say on this subject.

It is only left us now, after duly expounding the fashions of the torments of the Holy Martyrs treated of in this fourth chapter, to proceed next, with God's blessing, to the fifth.

CHAPTER V

Of Instruments wherewith the Heathen were used to tear the Flesh of Christ's Faithful Servants, to wit Iron Claws, Hooks, and Currycombs

THREE separate and distinct instruments were employed by the Devil-worshippers (as is attested by very many *Acts of the Martyrs*) for mangling Christians withal, namely iron claws, hooks, and currycombs. Of these the first sort are mentioned in many places of Tertullian, and particularly in his work *Against the Gnostics,* where he writes, "Some Christians they proved by fire, others by the sword, others by wild beasts ; yet others tasted martyrdom from cudgels and iron claws;"—likewise in his *Apology to the Heathen,* "You do set Christians on crosses and fix them to stakes. Tell me, what deformed likeness will not the clay assume, when set up on cross and stake ? On the gallows-tree is the body of your God first dedicated ; and with claws you scarify the sides of Christian martyrs," and again elsewhere, "Yes ! let claws pierce their flesh and crosses hang their bodies on high." So too St. Cyprian in the *Epistle to Donatus* saith, "Spear and sword and executioner are ready, and the claw that pricks and pierces," and in another place, "Now would the wooden horse rack them and the iron claw pierce." Also St. Gregory of Nyssen, in his *Life of St. Gregory Thaumaturgus*, "The posts were set up whereon the bodies of them that remained firm were stretched, and lacerated with horrible claws;" St. Augustine, *Letters*, "When he hath the open confession of such enormous crimes,—and this by no racking of the horse or ploughing of the iron claws;" St. Jerome, *Epistle to the Innocents*, "When the bloodstained claw was mangling the livid flesh, and pain was seeking to tear the truth from furrowed sides;" and the same Author a little further on, "Either side doth the executioner plough and furrow," that is with the iron claws. Prudentius in his Hymn of St. Romanus says—

Costas bisulcis execandas ungulis,

and lower down again—

Quam si cruenta membra carpant ungulae,

("Sides that must be cut open with the cloven claws," "An if the claws rend your bleeding limbs"); and elsewhere—

Ille virgas, secures, et bisulcas ungulas,

. . . .

Tormenta, carcer, ungulae,

("Rods, axes, and cloven claws . . . racks, prison, iron claws.")

Now these claws,—as is proven by one which is preserved to this day in the Church of St. Peter in the Vatican among the relics of the Saints, and which ourselves, though all unworthy, have seen, and kissed and venerated,—were a sort of iron pincers made as we shall now expound.

First, two longish pieces of iron were fastened together, just in the same way as those forming a smith's iron pincers are used to be joined and paired together. The ends of these were rounded and toward the extremities slightly hollowed, this being done to the end sundry little spears or spikes might be set and fixed therein, for the greater convenience of the tormentors mangling those set on the wooden horse or tied to stakes or hung up aloft, whether ordinary criminals or the Blessed Martyrs. This is plainly shown by a fragment of one of these spikes, half destroyed by heat and blunted, which is to be seen still fixed there. But in the upper parts, that is beginning from the junction of the two pieces of iron, they were one palm in length and two fingers in width, thin rather than thick, being of a slender and subtle construction. Moreover six iron points were attached to them, three on each, and so arranged that in the middle of one of them two points were firmly fixed in the surface of the metal, but in the middle of the other only one, facing the other two. Whence it came that when the pincers were closed, the one that stood single in the middle of the one piece met and interlocked with the two pricks on the other, entering in betwixt them, as it were. Nor was this all, for there were other similar sets of points fixed within the instrument's jaws (so to speak), the arrangement of the pricks being the same always. The result was that the flesh of such as were tormented with these same pincers or claws was torn and ploughed by the said points.

Fig. XVI.

A. Iron claws. | B. Currycombs, or heckles. | C. Hooks.

To face p. 106

Wherefore need it cause no surprise, if some of the authorities cited above have spoke of these instruments as *cloven* or two-furrowed, and have described them as cutting furrows, or ploughing the flesh of condemned criminals.

With this instrument of martyrdom were mangled and torn countless soldiers of Christ, and in especial Saints Papus, Clement of Ancyra, Theophilus and Theodorus, St. Maurice and his companions, Saints Justa, Rufina, Eulalia of Barcina, Saints Erasmus, Callinicus and Pelagius.

WHETHER THE PINCERS PRESERVED IN THE CHURCH OF ST. PETER BE MORE PROPERLY SCORPIONS OR IRON CLAWS.

Some there be have held this sort of iron pincers preserved in the Church of the Vatican among the relics of the Saints, as described above, to have been not *claws* at all, but *scorpions*. But an if we are to confess the real truth, we can only say such folk seem to us to be as far from the truth as the East is from the West. For indeed how can we possibly deem these pincers *scorpions* rather than *claws*, when,—as proven in the chapter next before this,—these (scorpions) were included under the name of rods, whereas these be described as a sort of iron toothed pincers? Moreover the former (as the *Acts of the Martyrs* and the passages of Holy Scripture quoted above indicate) were in use among the Ancients only for beating offenders withal, but the latter for mangling and rending the same. And this is confirmed by the shape and form of the said pincers, for to any one carefully considering the same it will at once be obvious they were never made for thrashing criminals, but for tearing and torturing them. For if the executioner took them in his hands with the intention of beating an offender, to carry out this purpose he would need to keep the two pieces of iron pressed together; and it would follow that the points, seeing they could in this wise torment no victim, must have been set and fixed there in vain and to no useful end whatever. We would add further that it is the proper function of claws (as St. Augustine and Prudentius have declared in their writings) to rend the flesh of delinquents and to tear and plough the same. And who can fail to see that these pincers preserved in the Church of St. Peter are excellently adapted to do this? There can be little or no doubt then that the said instrument belonged to the class of claws and no other sort whatever.

OF DIVERS INSTRUMENTS OF MARTYRDOM MADE OF IRON.

Having thus referred these claws to the class of iron pincers, we have now only to declare further, how many and what sorts there were in use for the tormenting of the Blessed Martyrs; for we know them to have been of many divers kinds. Some were toothed, and by means of six iron pricks did pierce the victim's skin, when closed together, and most cruelly rent and tare his limbs. Such were those we have just been speaking of. Others were specially made for crushing and twisting. Such are mentioned by Bishop Synesius, when treating in his *Letters* of the savage cruelty of the Governor Andronicus, he saith, "Unless with the pincers, an instrument contrived for pulling ears and twisting lips."

Others again were intended for cutting, of which sort mention is made in the *Roman Martyrology* under June 26th in these words, "At Cordova in Spain the anniversary of St. Pelagius, a young man who by reason of his confession of the Faith was ordered by Abdur-Rahman, King of the Saracens, to be cut limb from limb with iron pincers, and so did gloriously consummate his martyrdom."

In the same class of instruments of martyrdom may be included the pincers or scissors wherewith Christians of either sex, but more especially women, were shorn by the Servants of Devils by way of ignominy. See the *Acts* of St. John the Apostle, and the *History* of St. Fausta, virgin and martyr, and of St. Charitina, likewise virgin and martyr. To this day the pincers wherewith St. John the Evangelist was shorn be preserved in the most holy Church of St. John Lateran—a relic most deserving of visitation and reverence.

DIVERS FASHIONS WHEREIN THE MARTYRS WERE TORTURED WITH THE IRON CLAWS.

Divers were the fashions wherein Christians were mangled with the claws—sometimes bound on the wooden horse, or tied to stakes or pillars, sometimes hung up, at times with the head downward.

The first and second of these modes are attested by the *Acts* of Saints Nestor, Hilary, Justa and Rufina, Januarius and Pelagius, as also St. Maurice and his companions. The same is referred to likewise in what we have said above in Chapter I. on the subject of stakes; the last by the *Histories* of Saints Epimachus, Felix, and others already named. For further information read again what we have said in Chapter III. anent the word *Fidiculae.*

OF IRON HOOKS AS INSTRUMENTS OF MARTYRDOM.

Such hooks are mentioned by Cicero in his *Philippics,* " A hook was driven into that wretched runaway," and in the *Pro Rabirio,* " From lash and hook and terror of the cross neither our past history, our previous life, nor our honours availed to protect us." Also Juvenal in his *Satires* writes, ". . . *Sejanus ducitur unco* " ("Sejanus is dragged along with the hook of criminals ") ; and Horace, *Ode to Fortune* (i. 35)—

> *Te semper anteit saeva necessitas,*
> *Clavos trabales, et cuneos manu*
> *Gestans aena ; nec severus*
> *Uncus abest liquidumque plumbum.*

("Ever before thee goes harsh necessity, bearing in her brazen hand the spikes and wedges ; nor is the cruel hook wanting and the molten lead.") Again Suetonius, *Tiberius,* "When the executioner, as though by the Senate's authority, displayed before him ropes and hooks ; " and Lampridius, in his *Life of Commodus,* who says men shouted in scorn of that Emperor, when he was dead, " He who massacred the Senate, let him be dragged along by the hook ; he who massacred all men, let him be dragged along by the hook ; he who robbed the temples, let him be dragged along by the hook ! "—and so on, for indeed very frequent mention of the said hook is to be found in these writings. Similarly, writing of Vitellius,

Suetonius saith, "Eventually he was mangled with countless blows at the Gemonian steps and slain, and thence dragged with the hook to the Tiber;" and Ammianus Marcellinus, of the same Emperor, "The wooden horses were stretched, and the executioner was making ready the hooks," and again, "The hooks and bloody tortures." So too Prudentius in one of his *Hymns*—

Stridentibus laniatur uncis

("He is torn to pieces with the sounding hooks "). Also the *Acts* of St. Sebastian, where we read, "Search in the sewer that is near by the Great Circus, and there will you find my body hanging from a hook." Further mention is to be found of hooks in the *Histories* of other Martyrs, as Saints Plato, Pontianus, Nicetas, as also of Saints Tatiana, Martina, and Prisca, Roman Virgins and Martyrs.

From all which it is manifest how that the Ancients were used to employ hooks not only for mangling criminals or dragging them to the place of execution, that is to say the Gemonian steps, but likewise for hanging up the same aloft, and finally for dragging infamous malefactors, guilty of many abominations and crimes, which were now dead, to the sewers and receptacles of filth and refuse, or to the Tiber. Wherefore we need no more wonder when we find it writ concerning St. Sebastian, how that after his death his body was dragged with a hook to the Cloaca Maxima, a Great Sewer of Rome, seeing the Christians were esteemed by the Heathen as folk full of guilt and dishonour and as if born in dishonour. The hook then may be best described and defined thus, "It is a longish stick, or miniature spear, having an iron at one end, curved and bent back upon itself "—which instrument was in use among the Romans for haling condemned criminals to the Gemonian steps and for punishing the same, and lastly for dragging the dead bodies of evil men into the public sewers.

FASHIONS WHEREIN THE BLESSED MARTYRS WERE DRAGGED AND TORTURED WITH THE HOOK.

In precisely the same fashion were Christians tortured with the hook as they were with the iron claws mentioned above, as is proven (to omit other evidence) by the *Acts* of Saints Plato and Pontianus the martyrs just now referred to, and by what we have stated concerning stakes in Chapter I.

OF IRON CURRYCOMBS AS INSTRUMENTS OF MARTYRDOM.

For tearing of the flesh of faithful Christians iron combs were likewise applied. This is confirmed by the *Acts* of sundry martyrs, especially of St. Blase, Saints Tatiana, Julitta, and Barbara, virgins and martyrs, and a host of others whose names be known to God alone. These combs resembled, as their name and use do imply, and as shown by some represented in certain very ancient paintings of St. Blase, copied, as learned men judge, from drawings of the Ancients, these combs resembled, I say, those used to comb wool withal. To these combs was attached a small spear or staff of a convenient length, as was the case with the claws, for these likewise were used for mangling the martyrs. Thus do we see how three several instruments were framed for

Fig. XVII.

A. Martyr tortured by means of the iron claws or pincers.
B. Torn with the hooks.

C. Mangled with the iron currycombs.

To face p. 112

112a

rending the flesh of the Blessed Martyrs, to wit, claws, hooks, and combs of iron. Now as to the fashion wherein the victims were torn with these combs, it should be known that the Saints were martyred in precisely the same way with these as with the iron claws afore described.

OF SHARDS OR FRAGMENTS OF POTTERY USED FOR LACERATING THE FLESH OF THE SAINTS.

Sometimes was the Christians' flesh torn and rent by way of greater cruelty with fragments of pottery, to which end not only were their sides lacerated with the above-named articles, as was done with robbers, but their belly, thighs, and legs into the bargain. Listen, an you will, to Eusebius, who was an eye-witness of such cruelties, and hath pictured the fury of the tormentors in his *History* : "But of a truth it was in the Thebaid that all hitherto described cruelties were exceeded. For here the tormentors would take shards of pottery instead of claws and therewith tear and lacerate the whole body till they did scrape the skin from off the flesh ;" and again in another passage : "Now indeed was it held a usual and ordinary matter for a man to be ploughed and furrowed with the iron claws. But further, when this mode of torture was applied to any, not only were his sides (as is usually done to robbers and murderers) pierced and rent, but his belly likewise, and his thighs and legs. In fact the harrow was made to penetrate to his very marrow."

HOW THE SAINTS WERE STRETCHED TO THE FOURTH AND FIFTH HOLE OF THE STOCKS.

Not content with the aforesaid tortures wherewith they tormented the servants of Christ, the Devil's ministers daily pondered to discover fresh ways of cruelty and new sorts of punishment. And albeit they did discover many such, yet could they never succeed by their means in bending or breaking the divine valour of the Christians. Nay! rather did all these torments end in strengthening them the more and renowning them with more and more noble victories. The tyrant's cruelty might indeed torture and mangle their bodies, but their minds, fortified with celestial courage and celestial aid, they were in no wise able to weaken or overcome. Oh, happy, oh, blessed times! oh, fortunate beings! whose valour and whose virtue were such that even mere young boys in those days flinched under no torments, however terrible. These gallant athletes of Christ were torn and rent with iron claws and scourges; then for their more searching torture did these princes of darkness (see Eusebius, *Ecclesiastical History*) devise the torment of stretching them, when thus full of blows and wounds, in the stocks to the fourth or fifth hole. Yet when this was done, though they were in the most agonising pain, not a murmur nor a complaint was ever heard, for with steadfast and silent endurance these brave hearts were patient in adversity. But an if you would fain know more of this sort of torture refer back to what we have said thereanent in Chapter III., where we have shown how the wooden horse was one thing and the stocks another, and many other points relating to this matter.

CHAPTER VI

Of Red-hot Plates, and Torches, and Blazing Brands

FOR all the Heathen bade Christians of either sex, to the scorn of Christ, to be racked on the horse and mangled with scourges, iron claws, and the like (as hath been described in the preceding chapter), and to be stretched in the stocks to the fourth and fifth hole, yet was not their savage rage thereby exhausted. Whence it came that often and often they would have quicklime or molten lead or boiling oil or something similar poured over their fresh wounds, or else order the same to be torn open with shards of pottery or violently rubbed and scrubbed with hair cloths, or lastly, command the unhappy beings in this evil case to be horribly burned with red-hot plates, torches, and blazing brands.

OF RED-HOT OR FIERY PLATES.

Fiery Plates are spoke of by Plautus in his *Asinaria* in the words :— *Stimulos, laminas, crucesque*

("Goads, plates, and crosses "); by Cicero, *Against Verres :* "What, then, when the red-hot plates and other tortures were brought on the scene?" By Horace, *Epistles :—*

Scilicet ut ventres lamina candente nepotum
Diceret urendos correctus.

("So far reformed as to direct his grandsons' bellies to be scorched with the white-hot plate!") Also by St. Cyprian, *Praise of Martyrdom:* "For the Martyr's body is stretched on the rack and hissing to the red-hot plates." Prudentius in the *Hymn on the Martyrdom of St. Vincent:*—

Stridensque flammis lamina . . .

and again in that of St. Romanus :—

Nec inusta laminis ardet cutis

("And the plate hissing with fiery flames . . .;" "And the flesh burns scorched by the plates"); and lastly, Victor in the *Vandal Persecution:* "For then did Papinian, the venerable Bishop and Father of our City, have all his body burned with white-hot plates of iron."

The *Acts of the Blessed Martyrs* are full and overflowing with instances of this mode of torture, and Eusebius mentions it again and again, particularly in his *Ecclesiastical History.* In fact, such burning, when confined to the sides, was counted among common and public punishments.

Now a *plate* in this sense was (as sundry of the above quoted authorities and numerous *Histories* of the Holy Martyrs would seem to imply) a piece of any metal, longer than it was broad, and thicker than a layer or leaf. In fact, a layer or leaf doth herein differ from a plate that the former is thinner and will bend spontaneously, and crackles, whereas

FIG. XVIII.

A. Blazing brands or flambeaux.
B. Pine-wood and other torches.

C. Red-hot plates of metal.

To face p. 116

a plate is thicker and makes no crackling sound. For of it is armour made, and when heated red-hot, the same was used in old days for purposes of torture. Such a piece of iron heated in the fire was applied to the bare flesh of the Blessed Martyrs or of criminals, and there held till it had miserably burned the same. With this instrument of martyrdom were tortured those most glorious soldiers of Christ, St. Laurence, St. Bassus Bishop, St. Vincent, and many others.

Furthermore the *Theatre of Cruelties* doth show how in sundry cases the Heretics of our own day have done the like, and how Catholics even at the present time (1591) have been burned with fiery plates by the Huguenots and Calvinists.

OF TORCHES WHEREWITH THE BLESSED MARTYRS WERE BURNED.

Of suchlike torches mention is made in divers *Histories* of the Saints, especially in those of St. Saba, an officer of soldiers; of Saints Eulalia of Emerita and Barbara, virgins and martyrs; and of St. Clement, Bishop of Ancyra.

These torches, as used by the Ancients, were of two sorts,— some being made of the inner and denser parts of trees which produce resin, such as the pine, pitch-pine, larch, or fir. Such torches are often spoke of by Ancient writers, as by Varro, who writes: "Rome is alive with women; and what rites were used to be done at night-time, even now a pine torch indicates;" and again, "A torch is there, wrapped about with flame." So also Virgil, *First Georgic:—*

Ferro faces inspicat acutas

117

("He sharpens pointed torches with the knife"), where by torches the Commentators understand brands of pine wood; and again in the *Seventh Æneid:—*

Et castis redolent altaria tedis

("And the altars are fragrant with consecrated pine torches"). So too Cicero, "Rushing to and fro in terror of the Furies' blazing torches;" and in another speech, "Just as on the stage, Conscript Fathers, you see men, driven into crime by constraint of the gods, shudder in terror before the blazing torches of the Furies." Lastly, Suetonius, *Life of Nero:* "Often, the Emperor confessed, was he terrified by his mother's phantom, the whips of the Furies and their blazing torches."

So much for the first sort. Torches of the second kind were made of twisted coils of rope smeared with wax or pitch. These are mentioned by Virgil, *First Æneid:—*

Et noctem flammis funalia vincunt

("And torches disperse the darkness with their flames"); by Cicero, *De Senectute*, "His delight was in the torch of wax;" and again in the *De Officiis*, "Statues stood in every street, at which frankincense and torches of wax . . .;" and by Valerius Maximus, speaking of Caius Duilius, "Going to feast by the light of a torch of wax, with a flute-player preceding him."

This distinction being duly explained, we may add that torches of both these two sorts, to wit pine torches and torches of waxed or pitched rope, were used by the Heathen

FIG. XIX

A. Martyr hung from the wooden horse and scorched
   with the flame of torches.

B. Martyr suspended by the feet from a pulley and tortured in a like fashion.

To face p. 118

for scorching the Christians withal well-nigh to death. The use of pine torches is attested by the *Acts* of St. Barbara, virgin and martyr, above cited ; for where some have writ how that the Saint was burned with torches, others have recorded more particularly it was with pine torches she was tortured.

In fact both pine torches, and torches of the other sort, were greatly in use in those days, as the authors quoted seem to show, and as we should expect from the nature of things. For indeed the pitch-pine is more abundant in resin than the other trees which produce the same, more careful of that liquid and better adapted to give a pleasant flame (as Pliny saith) and supply light for sacred functions. Torches, there-fore, made of pitch-pine were more in use among the Ancients than any others of a like sort.

This form of torture is likewise,—as related in the *Theatre of Cruelties*,—employed by the heretics of our own day for afflicting the Catholics withal, and particularly by the Huguenots in their hatred of our holy religion, as may be read in that work.

OF BLAZING BRANDS, OR FLAMBEAUX.

Mention is made of burning brands,—which some do confound with torches, through want of due consideration of their true nature,—in sundry *Acts* of the Blessed Martyrs, as of Saints Theophilus, Felix and Fortunatus, Pantaleon, Regina virgin and martyr, Theodore a priest, Alexander a Bishop, Parmenius and his companions, and countless other holy martyrs.

These brands or flambeaux belong,—if we may trust certain representatives thereof to be seen here in Rome carven on *ancient* marbles,—to the same general class as torches, but were made in the following way. First, certain vessels were taken, a palm or span, or something over, in width across, which were then narrowed from the top or mouth to a gradually more and more contracted shape, like a pyramid reversed or turned upside down. These vessels were either of earthenware, as is shown by some that be from time to time dug up in the ruins of this city of Rome, or else of iron, as Columella states. Then afterward, these being enclosed with little staves of wood squared and tied together, and which like the vessels themselves were made finer and smaller from the top downward, were filled with fuel which gave off fire and flame. And these staves, if we consider the uses to which these flambeaux were put, we must conceive of as being some five or six spans long, more or less.

But that the instruments thus described by us from Ancient examples were flambeaux and not torches, that is torches of pine-wood, or of twisted coils of rope, is proven by many circumstances. In the first place it is to be noticed in the marbles before mentioned that the flame begins to burn more fiercely where the staves end, from which it follows they were not torches of the first kind, but of the second, to wit, brands or flambeaux ; for an if they *had* been ordinary torches, the staves, which acted as handles, being of wood, must obviously have been consumed by the fire contained in the vessels. Consider, moreover, that we never see any man fix wax tapers

FIG. XX.

A. Wooden horse.
B. Martyr taken down from the horse and being rolled about over shards of pottery.

C. Having quicklime, boiling oil and the like, poured over him.

To face p. 120

120a

burning all their length in candlesticks, but only at the end, that so they may the more conveniently burn and be consumed, and give a better light.

Some may perhaps make objection, and say there is nothing really to show they were not ordinary torches of the first sort, for that the staves or handles were not burned because they were of iron, and not of wood at all. But this cannot possibly have been the case, forasmuch as these brands or flambeaux were employed by the Ancients for scorching criminals when hoisted on the horse, or suspended aloft, or tied up to pillars or stakes, and must therefore be conceived as having been light rather than heavy, to the end the executioners might readily wield them in their hands ; so that we be bound to allow them to have been made of wood and not of iron. This view moreover is confirmed by the ensample of the iron claws or nippers afore named ; for these, though of no great weight, were yet attached to very light handles for the easier torturing of condemned persons.

It is clearly manifest then from these and other like considerations that these brands or flambeaux were divers and distinct from the ordinary torches first described ; and Virgil doth confirm the same by these verses in his *Ninth Æneid :—*

Princeps ardentem conjecit lampada Turnus,
Et flammam affixit lateri, quae plurima vento
Corripuit tabulas, et postibus haesit adesis.

(" First Turnus hurled a blazing brand and touched the flank with flame, that fanned to fury by the wind seized on the planks and clave to the doorposts, which it began to gnaw away.")

Tortures and Torments of the Christian Martyrs

OF THE FASHION WHEREIN THE MARTYRS WERE BURNED AND SCORCHED WITH FIERY BRANDS.

In just the same fashion were the Blessed Martyrs burned and scorched with these fiery brands as they were tortured by means of iron claws, currycombs and hooks,—as is testified by many of the *Acts* of the Martyrs above quoted and the details we have already given in Chapter I. concerning pillars, trees and stakes as employed in torturing Christ's servants.

OF TORMENTS WHEREWITH THE MARTYRS WERE TORTURED AFTER BEING TAKEN DOWN FROM THE HORSE.

Lastly it must be noted how these same servants of Christ, after being taken down from off the wooden horse, were then tortured with the divers instruments described above, or else racked and stretched and their legs drawn asunder in the stocks to the fourth or fifth hole (as related in Chapter III.), or rolled naked over shards of pottery, or even sometimes drenched with boiling oil or the like.   These torments, all and sundry, are proven by the *Acts* of the Blessed Martyrs,—as in the case of St. Vincent and St. Pelagius, of St. Felix and St. Fortunatus.   Nay! there be yet other sufferings we read of inflicted on those taken down from the horse, whereof constant mention is made in divers other *Acts* of the Holy Martyrs, for the which consult, an you will, the History of St. Menna in particular.—But enough said of torches, red-hot plates and burning brands.

CHAPTER VII

Of the Brazen Bull, Frying-pan, Pot, Caldron, Gridiron, and Bedstead; likewise of the Chair, Helmet, and Tunic, and other Instruments of Martyrdom of Red-hot Iron

IN the preceding chapter we have treated of divers instruments of martyrdom wherewith condemned persons were burned; it doth only remain here to discuss certain others wherewith the same or a like manner of torture was inflicted. Accordingly we will begin with the Brazen Bull, a most exceeding cruel sort of punishment in use among the Ancients, into the which (as the *Acts* of the Martyr St. Eustachius show, as well as the Dialogue of Lucian, entitled *Phalaris*) anyone that was to be tortured was cast by an opening or door that was in its side. Then the door being shut to again, a fire was lighted about the bull, causing those imprisoned therein to suffer unexampled agonies, and by their lamentations and cries to imitate the bellowing of a bull. And this brazen contrivance was so cunningly wrought to the likeness of a real bull that (as Lucian doth attest in the *Dialogue* named) movement and voice alone were lacking to persuade folk it was a living animal.

Now the inventor of the said engine (so Ovid saith in the *Tristia*) was a certain Athenian, a man of superior cleverness, Perillus by name. Thinking he would be doing a great favour to Phalaris, the Tyrant of Agrigentum, as one which did ever delight in novel tortures and was used to find his chief pleasure in inflicting cruel punishments, he was sore deceived in the hope wherein he trusted. For by the Despot's order, from whom he was expecting no small guerdon, he was thrown himself into the bull and offered the first example of the working of his own invention. Whereof Ovid hath sung in these words following :—

Et Phalaris tauro violenti membra Perilli
Torruit ; infelix imbuit auctor opus.

("And Phalaris roasted Perillus' limbs in the cruel bull; the ill-starred inventor was first to hansel his own handiwork ") ; and Propertius :—

Et gemere in tauro, saeve Perille, tuo.

("And to groan, cruel Perillus, in the bull you invented "). To these passages we may likewise add what Valerius Maximus hath to say of Perillus and his cruel device : "Then there was that cruel inventor of the brazen bull wherein men were shut up and fires kindled underneath, so that they were constrained by the long-drawn, though unseen, torment to utter resounding cries, which took on the form of mere bellowings, that their wails of agony might not, being expressed in human voice and language, appeal to the pity of the Tyrant Phalaris.

Now forasmuch as he was fain to rob the miserable victims of all hope of pity, the artist was the first to be imprisoned in the bull and deservedly to try the dreadful effects of his own device."

But an if you be fain to know more of this, read the *Letters* (Pseudo-letters) of Phalaris, Cicero, *Against Piso, Pliny,* Ovid's *Tristia,* and especially Lucian in the Dialogue entitled *Phalaris.* Yet in this last there is a certain admixture of pure invention ; for it is there pretended that Perillus' bull was sent by Phalaris to Delphi to be consecrated in the Temple of Apollo among other offerings to the god, but inasmuch as all men deemed him a most cruel and abominable Tyrant, the gift was like to be refused at the holy place as coming from an impious evil-doer, and that to guard against its rejection, he caused his ambassadors in a speech crammed full of lies to contradict the commonly received report of these atrocities.

Nay! more, not only did Perillus make experience of his own contrivance, but so did Phalaris himself. For the time came when his exceeding and overbearing violence could no more be borne, and the citizens of Agrigentum making common cause against him, he was seized, shut up in the same bull wherein he had burned others, and roasted alive.

Ovid hath commemorated his fate in the lines :—

Utque ferox Phalaris, lingua prius ense resecta,
More bovis Phario clausus in aere gemas:

("And like cruel Phalaris, the tongue first cut out with the sword and imprisoned in Egyptian brass, may you groan and bellow like a bull.")

Valerius Maximus, however, would seem to think differently as to the mode of this Tyrant's death, for he writes : "By his fierce invectives against their cowardice and want of enterprise Zeno so roused the Agrigentines to a sudden fury and determination that they set on Phalaris and stoned him ; " and Cicero, *De Officiis,* doth pretty much agree with him, "Phalaris was renowned above all mankind for cruelty, who perished not in an ordinary revolt, but by a general uprising against him of the whole population of Agrigentum." Yet may we reconcile the divers statements of Ovid on the one hand and of Valerius Maximus on the other, if we suppose the Tyrant was first attacked with stones, and afterwards cast into the red-hot brazen bull.

Beside these, many others likewise endured this form of punishment, whereof some did profess the Christian Faith ; for indeed such was the rage and fury wherewith the Heathen did assail Christ's faithful servants, that they did resuscitate and employ for their destruction all sorts of excessively cruel, but antiquated and old-fashioned, instruments of Martyrdom. Now Christians which were cast into the brazen horse and there shut up to die were Saints Antipas, Saint Eustachius, a Roman patrician, his wife, Theopistes, and his sons Agapius and Theopistus, and St. Pelagia, virgin and martyr, all of whom (as their *Acts* do loudly proclaim) sprang lightly and with alacrity into the red-hot monster. For they did enter the same,—Antipas rendering fervent thanks to God,

FIG. XXI.

A. Martyr roasting on the iron framework or gridiron. | B. Iron shovel for stirring the fire of coals.

To face p. 126

Eustachius along with wife and sons exulting in exceeding great joy, while Pelagia, the virgin of Tarsus, sang with great gladness an Hymn of Triumph to God.

Furthermore, we read of some other Christian martyrs which were imprisoned in the brazen bull, but by the Divine grace protecting them, came forth thereof safe and unharmed. Amongst these was a certain soldier, St. Barbarus by name, and St. Heliodorus, the latter of whom is thus commemorated under December 1: "Anniversary of the Blessed Martyr Heliodorus of Maghedo, a city of Pamphilia. Aurelian being Emperor of Rome and Aëtius Governor in the city of Maghedo in Pamphilia, St. Heliodorus for preaching of Christ in the said city was brought before the Governor. Whereupon, when he would not endure to make sacrifice to idols, he was instantly hung up and thrashed ; and when he felt the bitterness of the torment, he cried out, 'Lord Jesu Christ, help me.' And at once he heard a voice from heaven saying, 'Fear not, I am with thee.' This was heard of them which were holding the torches ready lighted to burn him withal, and these and four beside, which saw Angels staying the torments, believed on Christ, and remonstrating with the Governor, were thrown into the sea and so received the crown of victory. Then did the Governor command the brazen bull to be heated and the Martyr to be cast therein ; but no sooner was this done than by his prayers the monster which was red-hot grew instantly cold. And the Judge was the more astonied thereat, because he heard the man singing of psalms inside. Going therefore to the brazen engine and seeing it at one moment shooting out sparks, at the next turned suddenly cold again, he did rebuke the Saint, saying, 'Thou wicked sinner! hast by thy magic arts prevailed against the fire?' To which the holy man made answer, 'Nay! my magic arts are Christ! But give me three days' time to think over in my heart what I must do.' Receiving accordingly this respite, he betook him secretly to the Temple of the gods, and lo! when he had made a prayer to the true God, all the idols suddenly fell down and brake in pieces. But when the Governor heard therefore, he was filled with fury and ordered Heliodorus to be brought before him, and then hanged, and nails heated red-hot to be driven into his head. Presently when the Judge saw how the Martyr was still unconquered, whatever the number and diversity of torments he endured, he sent him away to the city of Atala, where, remaining constant in his profession of the Faith, he was set in a hot frying-pan, where he stood and prayed, continuing all the while unhurt. Whereupon all the bystanders believed on the Lord, crying, 'A great God verily is the God of the Christians.' So when the Governor saw many folk converted to believe in Heliodorus' God, fearing they might rescue him from out his hands, he ordered him to be carried back again to Maghedo, whither the guards led him praying and singing psalms. Then was the Saint a second time questioned, but only continued the more steadfast in his former confession of Jesus Christ. The Governor next commanded his tongue to be cut out, and that he should be hung up and scourged by the space of two hours. So after putting a collar on him, they dragged him forth of the city. But the holy man

signed to them with his hand, and stood still to preach ; and
when his sermon was ended, he was cut to pieces."—So far, so
good ; and now to proceed to the next division of our subject.

OF THE BRAZEN POT AS AN INSTRUMENT OF MARTYRDOM.

This is mentioned both in Holy Scripture, in the *Book of
the Maccabees*, and by Josephus in his work on the same
subject, as likewise in the *Acts* of the Saints, especially those
of St. Boniface, St. Juliana, and St. Lucy. A pot was a very
capacious vessel made of brass, into the which condemned
persons were stripped and thrown, to be boiled or seethed
therein.

Now you should know that the Ancients were used to
employ many and divers sorts of vessels for the torturing of
offenders, and particularly of Christians. For they had
frying-pans for lightly roasting or frying their flesh, caldrons
and pots for throughly boiling or seething the same. Now
these pots were nothing more nor less than ordinary kitchen
pots for boiling meat withal, as is indicated by the word itself,
as well as by the references made to the thing in many
Ancient authors, as for instance by Varro : "To spin wool,
and at the same time keep an eye on the pot, that the pottage
be not burned ; " by Plautus, *Amphitryon :*—

Optimo jure infringatur olla cineris in caput

("He well deserves a pot of ashes be broken over his head ") ;
and by Persius in his *Fourth Satire :*—

Caepe et farratam, pueris plaudentibus, ollam

("Bring out, amid the clapping of the lads, onions and the pot of pottage").

These pots, then (as said above), were very large vessels made of brass, wherein the martyrs were boiled as a punishment at once terrible and ignominious. They were fashioned (as is proven by very ancient examples often dug up from the ruins of this city of Rome) in the likeness of the pots we commonly use for cooking food, without rims, but having two handles, which were part square, part round,—square from the bottom to the middle, round from the middle upwards to the brim, or else made on the model of a pair of ears. On the other two sides they had two partly hollow projections of iron facing one another, wherein rings, likewise of iron, were fitted, to the end the tormentors might more easily lift the same and carry them where they would. All this will be found more plainly and particularly shown in the pot which we have had drawn from ancient examples to be seen in Figure XXII.

DIVERS WAYS IN WHICH THE SERVANTS OF ALMIGHTY GOD WERE PUT INTO THE POT.

Sometimes were the followers of God plunged into a pot head downwards; as we read in the *Acts* of the Martyr St. Boniface : "Then the Judge in a passion ordered a pot to be brought and filled with boiling pitch, and the holy martyr,—St. Boniface to wit,—to be cast into it head first. So the blessed martyr of Christ, after signing the sign of the cross, was plunged into the pot." Moreover, in other cases

FIG. XXII.

A. Martyr thrown head-first into a caldron full of molten
   lead or boiling oil.

B. Martyr in a hot frying-pan.
C. Martyr plunged into a boiling pot.

To face p. 130

victims were thrown into the pot so squeezed together in the press and doubled up that their head was made to touch their knees. This second fashion is attested by Josephus in the words following : "He is put by the executioners' hands into the pot,—such is the name given to this form of criminal punishment. The press being turned or revolved, his holy head is forced to his knees, and his body being thus reduced in height, the champion of the Faith was squeezed miserably into the aforesaid pot."

The reader should here observe that by *the press* Josephus denoted some instrument for pressing or squeezing,—not, however, so much the great press or beam wherewith grapes and olives are crushed and pressed, but rather a smaller engine for pressing, such as fullers, paper-makers, and printers do chiefly use. Thus Pliny saith, speaking of divers kinds of paper, "Then are they squeezed in the presses and dried in the sun, and the several sheets joined together."

OF THE CALDRON.

There was yet another sort of vessel used by the Ancients (as the *Histories* of the Martyrs bear witness) for boiling the Christians withal, to wit a very large brazen caldron, which was filled with boiling oil or pitch, molten lead or wax, and the like, and the victims cast therein. This we do often read of in the *Acts* of the Blessed Saints, in particular those of Saints Saba and Zeno, and St. Veneranda, virgin and martyr. We hear of such a caldron again in the *Book of the Maccabees* (Chapter VII.) and in Josephus' *History of the Wars of the Maccabees.* As to its shape, this appears, to omit other references, sufficiently indicated by the lines in Ovid's *Metamorphosis :*—

> *Vina dabant animos, et prima pocula pugna,*
> *Missa volant, fragilesque cadi, curvique lebetes.*

("Wine stirs their spirit, and the fight begins with hurling flying cups and fragile jars and rounded caldrons.")

In both these vessels were tortured great numbers of Christ's soldiers,—in pots, Saints Boniface, Juliana, Lucy, Erasmus ; in caldrons, St. Zeno, St. Veneranda virgin and martyr, Saints Saba, Marianus, Pantaleëmon, Eulampius and his sister Eulampia, Zenobius and Zenobia, brothers and sisters.

OF THE FRYING-PAN AS AN INSTRUMENT OF TORTURE.

Mention is made of the frying-pan in the *Second Book of the Maccabees* (Chap. VII.) and in very many collections of the *Acts* of the Blessed Martyrs, as of St. Eleutherius the Bishop, Saints Fausta and Justina, virgins and martyrs.

The frying-pan,—if we may trust the natural meaning of the word and the afore-named *Histories* of the Blessed Martyrs,— was a wide open dish or plate, which (as the *Acts* of the Martyrs bear witness) was filled with oil, pitch, resin or sulphur, and then set over a fire ; and when it began to boil and bubble, then were Christians of either sex thrown into it, such as had persisted steadfastly and boldly in the profession of Christ's faith, to the end they might be roasted and fried like fishes cast into boiling oil. So in the *Hymn of St. Romanus* we find Prudentius writing as follows concerning one of the seven Maccabees brothers which was tortured in this way :—

Videbat ipsos apparatus funerum
Praesens suorum, nec movebatur parens,
Laetata, quoties aut olivo stridula
Sartago frixum torruisset puberem.

("The mother was present, gazing on all the preparations for her dear one's death and showed no sign of grief, rejoicing rather each time the pan hissing hot above the olive wood roasted and scorched her child.")

But as concerning its shape, we may believe it to have been round ; for as experience shows and the very use of the article dictates, all vessels that we use for seething or frying, or for boiling water in, are circular. Nor can it really be doubted but the vessels in use to-day have come down to us from the examples of the Ancients, albeit the modern be more perfectly made than their models,—seeing it is easy to add improvements to existing inventions. Moreover, some very old vessels are to be found that have remained uninjured, and be still intact, to this day, and these have identically the same shape as ours, as is attested by the pots, pitchers and like vessels that be sometimes dug up from the ruins of Rome. One of these is to be seen to this day in the Church of St. Laurence beyond the Walls, that wherein that most gallant champion of Christ, St. Laurence, did baptise a certain soldier of the Emperor's guard, Romanus by name.

So, seeing the vessels we now use have come down to us from those of the Ancients, which were very much like our own, it doth follow that the frying-pan, whereof we are speaking now, was of circular shape. Besides which, Ancient writers in describing their vessels have used expressions which prove this beyond a doubt, as is manifest from the passage of Ovid above quoted. We may say positively then that the frying-pan among the old Romans was of circular shape.

FASHION WHEREIN THE MARTYRS WERE TORTURED IN THE FRYING-PAN.

In two divers fashions were Christian Martyrs roasted in the frying-pan. Sometimes they were cast bodily into the same, with faces looking heavenward; and in these cases, because there must be some proportion kept betwixt the instrument of torture and the man tortured therein, I should conjecture they were thrown into a frying-pan which was rather an oval than a perfect round. Other times (as witnessed by the *Acts* of St. Euphemia) they were not set bodily therein, but limb by limb. And this is so stated expressly in the account of the holy virgin St. Euphemia, where we read, "Priscus the Proconsul commanded her to be divided limb from limb with knives, and the severed members to be roasted in a frying-pan. . . ." Now in this case it would seem likely, and we will pronounce it likely, that the frying-pan was of the round variety.

Further, the reader will observe how that the Blessed Martyrs, when roasting in the pan, were forced down therein

FIG. XXIII.

A. Martyr's dismembered limbs put in a frying-pan.
B. Martyr in the brazen bull.

C. Laid on the iron bed and broiled.

To face p. 134

134a

by means of iron forks; for indeed the purpose of the iron framework or gridiron and of the frying-pan seems to have been one and the same, both of them being used for burning Christians to death. So just as martyrs which were broiled on the gridiron were used to be held down on it by the executioners (as stated in the *Acts* of St. Laurence) with iron forks, similarly they that were tortured in the frying-pan may be surely assumed to have been crushed down and held therein in the same way.

OF THE GRIDIRON, AND IRON BED.

Having thus examined the instruments wherewith the Christian martyrs were boiled or fried, we have now only to turn our discourse upon those whereby their flesh was broiled by their heathen tormentors. These were the gridiron and the iron bed, of both of which frequent mention is found in the divers *Acts* of the Blessed Martyrs.

Gridirons are spoke of in the *Histories* of numerous Saints, as of Saints Eleutherius, Conon and Dulas, of St. Domna virgin and martyr, and of St. Laurence; iron beds in the *Acts* of the same St. Eleutherius, as likewise in those of the most sainted Clement of Ancyra, Plato, and others.

But to return to the iron frame or gridiron, its nature is sufficiently indicated both by the name, the aforesaid *Histories* of the Saints, and the gridiron whereon the most Holy Confessor of Christ, St. Laurence, was broiled, and which is religiously preserved, part of it in the Church of St. Laurence in Lucina, part at Paneperna. It was framed of three iron bars set lengthwise and a span distant one from the other, one finger thick, two broad, and of a length suitable for its purpose, with seven or more shorter pieces of iron placed crosswise, and likewise separated a span from each other. Of these some were round, some square, the square ones being the two which were joined to the ends of the longitudinal bars to brace together and strengthen the whole gridiron. There were likewise fixed at each corner and in the middle supports, also of iron, raising the framework a little off the ground and serving as legs.

We do not imagine that all gridirons were made with only three bars lengthwise, but only some; for we read in the *Acts* of St. Laurence how the Emperor commanded an iron framework of three bars to be brought for the burning of the holy man, from which it doth follow that such were to be found among the Ancients both with three and with more bars.

MARTYRS WHICH WERE ROASTED ON THE GRIDIRON.

The following were tortured on the gridiron, whereon they were held down with iron forks, and so roasted with fire laid underneath: Saints Laurence, Dulas, Eleutherius, Conon, Dorotheus, Macedonius, Theodulus, Tatian, and Peter. This last we find commemorated under March 12th in these words following :—"At Nicomedia the martyrdom of the Blessed Peter. Being Chamberlain to the Emperor Diocletian, he remonstrated over freely concerning the excessive torments the Christian martyrs were made to endure.

Wherefore by his master's order he is brought before him and hung up and beat for a very long while with scourges, then rubbed with vinegar and salt, and finally broiled on a gridiron over a slow fire. Thus was he inheritor at once of St. Peter's faith and name." Yet other facts concerning this same holy martyr will be found writ in the *Acts* of those most glorious soldiers of Christ, Saints Dorotheus and Gorgonius. These be now in manuscript, but we hope by God's gift soon to edit and print the same, together with numberless other *Histories* of Saints of either sex never before published. This task accomplished, we do propose further, if life be spared us, to write careful notes upon the several Lives of the Saints thus far published, wherein we shall endeavour, so far as in us lies, to distinguish what is true and certain from what is doubtful or found to be positively untrue.

So much for the gridiron, from which another instrument called in the *Acts* of the Blessed Martyrs the Iron Bedstead was altogether distinct. For in the *History* of St. Eleutherius, Bishop and Martyr,—mentioned a little above,—we read how the Tyrant which was ordering him to be tortured did direct the said holy man, after he had been tormented by his command on an iron bed, to be removed therefrom and roasted on an iron grid, which showeth beyond a doubt the iron bed to have been entirely distinct from the gridiron. But for the completer satisfaction of the reader, we think it best to cite the very words of the account, as follows :—"Then Hadrian, boiling with rage, ordered the brazen bed to be brought, and commanded the man to be laid thereon and bound legs and arms to the four corners, that his tender limbs might be stretched and racked. This done, fire was set underneath. . . . But when an hour was passed, the Emperor, thinking he was dead, ordered the bands to be loosed. Then stretching out his hands, he said to the Romans, 'Great is the Lord of the Christians, whom those most blessed saints, Peter and Paul, did preach to us, who performed many signs and wonders in this city and struck down to the earth that notorious Simon Magus, which did glorify and worship the same devils as Hadrian also doth.' Then did the Emperor order the gridiron to be smeared with oil and brought in, and commanded fire to be set underneath. . . ." This from the *Acts* of St. Eleutherius, whereby we do clearly gather that the gridiron was a different thing from the iron bed. This is further confirmed by what is writ concerning the same holy man in the *Roman Martyrology* under April 18th, as follows :—"At Messina, anniversary of the Blessed Martyrs, St. Eleutherius, Bishop of Illyricum, and St. Anthia, his mother. Illustrious for the holiness of their life and wonder of their miracles, they did under Hadrian overcome the pangs of the iron red-hot bedstead, the gridiron and the frying-pan boiling with oil, pitch, and resin. . . ." This doth again show the gridiron was distinct from the iron bed. Now this latter (as is attested by the *Acts* of the Martyrs) was made in the likeness of a real bedstead, oblong and raised somewhat from the earth for convenience in serving the fire underneath, with a number of iron bars carried across from side to side to take the place of the usual planks, leaving a space betwixt each.

FIG. XXIV.

A Martyr whose hand is filled with incense mingled with live coals, and who being constrained by the pain to scatter the incense, is said to have made sacrifice to the idol.

B. Martyr clad in the iron tunic and shod with the red-hot shoes, which consume the flesh from off his bones.

C. Martyr seated in the iron chair, while a red-hot helmet, or morion, is set on his head.

D. Martyr whose eyes are burned out with a lighted brand.

To face p. 138

These be the names of the most glorious martyrs which were tortured on the iron bed,—Saints Eleutherius, Clement of Ancyra, Plato, of whom we have already spoke, likewise Saints Olympiades, Maximus, Pegasius, and many others, whose names and numbers God alone knoweth.

OF THE CHAIR, HELMET, TUNIC, AND OTHER INSTRUMENTS OF IRON HEATED RED-HOT.

Besides these iron frames and bedsteads, the Heathen did likewise use for tormenting Christians withal the iron chair heated red-hot. This is testified by the *Acts* of Saints Paul and Juliana, by St. Gregory of Nyssa in the Life he writ of St. Gregory Thaumaturgus, and likewise by the History of Saint Blase, wherein is the following: "Again the Judge commanded seven seats of brass to be brought in, and bade the women, seven in number, which during the tormenting of St. Blase had collected the drops of his blood as they fell, to sit thereon, one in each. Then were the said seats heated so hot that sparks flew from them as from a furnace heated to the utmost."

But we must go on now to the red-hot helmets, wherewith the Christians were likewise tortured; for it was an habit and established custom among the Heathen to cover their heads with these on occasion. This is proven by the *History* of the martyrdom of St. Clement of Ancyra and that of St. Justus, a soldier, where is writ under July 14, "The day of trial of the Holy Martyr St. Justus, who was of the city of Rome, a soldier serving under the Tribune

Claudius. Returning once from a victory over the Barbarians, he saw a cross appearing before him like a crystal, and heard a voice issuing therefrom. Instructed by it in the mystery of godly piety, he did distribute on arriving at Rome all his goods to the poor, exulting in the faith of Christ. But when this came to the ears of the Tribune, and Christ's martyr would in no wise deny the profession he had made, he sent him to the Governor Magnentius. Questioned by him and found constant in his steadfastness to the Christian faith, he was ordered to be scourged with whips of raw hide, and afterward to have his head capped with a fiery helmet, and iron balls heated red-hot to be put under his armpits. All these torments and others of a like kind the Blessed Martyr bare unflinchingly, blessing God the while, and was finally cast into a furnace, where he gave up the ghost, albeit his sacred body did remain whole and unconsumed, not a hair of his head being hurt by the fire whereinto he was thrown." So much then for the fiery helmet.

But we must not think that the fury of the Heathen was glutted by these dreadful tortures inflicted on the holy martyrs, or that their cruelty was therefore slackened against Christ's servants. Rather was their rage more inflamed thereby to devise daily for their savage torment other new and horrible sorts of punishment. Thus were they clothed in the iron burning tunic, as we read of St. Erasmus; or their temples were pierced with red-hot nails, as is writ concerning the martyrs, Saints Victoricus and Fulcianus; or they were burned under the armpits and sides by means of iron spikes heated to a great heat, as befell St. Taracus and his companions; or else they were made to wear shoes of red-hot brass, as is told of St. Antymus, Bishop of Nicomedia, or compelled to walk shod in iron shoes nailed on with red-hot nails. Thus we find it writ under May 22, concerning the Blessed Martyr, St. Basiliscus, "Day twenty-second, anniversary of St. Basiliscus, martyred under the Emperor Maximian, from the district of Amasea. Imprisoned on account of his profession of Christ's faith by Agrippa the Governor, he was repeatedly shod with iron shoes nailed on with red-hot nails, and ordered to be driven along the road leading to Comana. And when on the way they had come to a certain place where dwelt a woman named Trojana, they did bind the holy man, his hands tied behind his back, to a barren plane-tree, the which tree the Saint, by praying to God, made green again, and caused a fountain suddenly to bubble forth from the ground. And seeing these things, the soldiers and the woman all believed in Jesus Christ. Moreover when he reached the City of Comana, and could in no wise be induced to make sacrifice, he prayed to God, which sent down fire from heaven and burned up the Temple and idol of Apollo. At this the Governor was sore angered, and commanded the Martyr Basiliscus to be cut to pieces and cast into the river. Thus did he win the crown of martyrdom, to the praise and glory of Almighty God." But enough said of this particular sort of instrument of torture.

CHAPTER VIII

Of Divers other Fashions wherein Christ's Holy Martyrs were Tortured with Fire

DAY by day and all day long was the Devil, the Prince of Darkness and Father of Lies, busy teaching the idolatrous Emperors and their ministers fresh fashions wherein, over and above the modes described already, they might torture Christ's servants with new and ever new torments. Whence it came that some of them were forced to walk barefoot over a floor strewn with live coals, of whom were St. Tiburtius, a most noble Roman, and St. Pontianus ; while others again were thrown into the fire to be burned. In this way was gained the crown of martyrdom by St. Polycarp, Saints Theodora, Euphrosyna, Flavia Domitilla, St. Fructuosus a Bishop, Saints Aubonia and Theophila virgins and martyrs, beside twenty thousand Christians, whereof we are told in the Greek *Menology*, under December 28, in these words, "The day of trial of the twenty thousand saints which were martyred under the Emperor Maximian, being burned to death at Nicomedia."

Furthermore, at Satan's instance were Christ's faithful followers sometimes burned in body or head with coals of fire, or these were put alight into their mouths or ears, or else the holy martyrs would be bound down on iron beds, and molten lead, boiling oil, blazing pitch, wax, sulphur, and similar substances poured over their limbs. These torments, all and several, are attested in the *Histories* of very many noble martyrs, for instance, of Saints Agapitus, Timothy, Apollinaris, Pelagius, Victor a soldier, Felix and Fortunatus, Boniface, Claudius and his companions, and an host of others.

Yet was not the Devil content with these torments inflicted of yore upon Christian men, but did further cause Christ's martyrs to be rolled back and forth, stripped of their clothes, over sharp shards and burning coals to their exceeding pain, or else force them to hold live coals, placed in their hands along with incense, before the altars of idols, so that, an if they should chance to toss down the burning embers, they might thus seem to have offered incense to the false gods of the Heathen. The first of these forms of torture is attested in the *Acts* of Saints Firmus and Rusticus and Saints Agatha and Macra, virgins and martyrs; the second in the *Histories* of the martyrdom of St. Procopius, as also of St. Cyrilla, virgin, who is commemorated under July 5th in these words:—"Commemoration of the blessed martyr, St. Cyrilla, which lived under the Emperors Diocletian and Maximian and belonged to the city of Cyrené in Libya. She was accused before Dignianus the Governor, and stood for judgment along with Lucia and Roa, two pious women. And when she could not be induced to make offering to idols, live coals were put in her hands and incense, and she was forced to sacrifice. But

she cried aloud, 'This enforced act is not to pay sacrifice.'
So when her fingers were consumed, she was then hung up
and scourged, and presently when she was taken down from
the stake, blood did flow from her wounds and milk from her
breast like a torrent, and so this blessed Saint and Martyr
gave up her spirit to God."

Another thing we would have you know, reader, is how the
Emperor Julian, called the Apostate, was used to cajole
Christian soldiers of his army by promising them gifts, an if
they made offering of incense for the fire on the day of the
Imperial distribution of largess. This is attested by St.
Gregory Nazianzen, who writes in his first Invective against
the said Emperor as follows :—

" Now the day of the Imperial largess was come, whether the
actual birthday (of Julian the Apostate), or so fixed for that date
with that Emperor's usual cunning artfulness, and all soldiers
were bound to present themselves, to the end each, according to his proper rank and dignity, might receive a donative.
Once more the same scene of sordid greed, the same tale of
impiety. Anxious to veil his cruelty under an aspect of good-
natured liberality, the Emperor endeavoured to entice and
allure with gifts of money the foolish pride and avarice of the
soldiers,—qualities that always play a great part in their lives.
So there sat the Prince presiding in state, holding high holiday
against goodness and piety, and not a little elate at the
cunning of his own devices. You might have deemed him
a Melampus or a Proteus, so ready was he to follow any course
or take on any shape or form. But what doings went on about

FIG. XXV.

A. Martyr tortured by means of red-hot irons under the armpit.
B. Roasted on live coals.

C. Martyr over whom boiling pitch is being poured, or the like substances.

To face p. 114

him, deserving of what sore grief and disapproval by all men
of sense,—not alone such as were there present, but all which
do hear of the spectacle by report. There was gold on one
hand, incense on the other, while fire was ready close at hand
and men standing by to urge compliance. Indeed it was a
plausible tale enough,—it was the regular custom of the
Imperial largess, an old and time-honoured ceremonial.
What was it? merely to set the incense alight,—yea! and so
earn the wages of death at the Emperor's hand, to accept how
small a payment for how great a sacrifice, the loss of their
souls and an act of direct impiety against Almighty God!

"A wretched guerdon truly, a poor recompense! The
whole army was put up for sale, cajoled by one and the same
vile trick; the soldiers which had conquered the world with
their arms were undone for a little fire and gold and a puff of
incense smoke, the most of them,—and this was the most
grievous point of all,—not even knowing their own ruin. A
man came forward, hoping to make a little gain; and for gain
he lost his own soul. He kissed the Emperor's hand,—and
knew not that he was greeting his own executioner. Nor
even if they did see this, were they any the better for the fact,
seeing they were once caught in the snare and held their
stupid acquiescence as a law that could in no wise be broken.
What myriads of Persians, what hosts of bowmen and
slingers, what army in panoply of steel, invulnerable on every
side, what engines for battering down the walls of cities,
could have brought about a result which one hand and one
occasion added to evil purpose easily affected?

"At this point I will intersperse a little story, sadder and more pitiful than those above. It is said that some of them which had been caught and cajoled in ignorance, returning after being thus unwittingly involved in disaster, sat down to meat with their comrades in barracks; then presently, when the meal had come to the customary draught of cold water, just as if nothing serious had happened to alter their condition, they lifted up their eyes, as was their wont, and invoked Christ with the sign of the cross. But one of their comrades marvelling at this, asked, 'Why, what is this? Do you invoke Christ after abjuring Him?' Startled at this question, they exclaimed, 'Nay! How have we abjured Him? What is this strange thing you say?' But the other answered, 'Why, by offering incense for the fire; what else is this, pray, but denying Christ?' Then did they, without an instant's delay, spring up from table, and like madmen and lunatics, boiling with zeal and indignation, rush through the Forum shouting out these words, 'Christians, Christians are we at heart; let all men hear us say so, and most chiefly God, for whom we live and are ready to die. The pledge we gave Thee, Christ our Saviour, we have not broken; our holy profession we have not abjured. If our hand hath offended, our intention never certainly went with it. We have been cajoled by the Emperor's trick, not contaminated with gold. We wash our hands of the wickedness, and will purge ourselves with blood.' And afterward going quickly to the Emperor, and boldly and defiantly casting down the gold, they cried out in these terms: 'It is not gifts we have

Fig. XXVI.

Martyr compelled to walk over burning coals, while molten lead, boiling pitch, or the like substances, are poured over his head.

To face p. 146

received, Emperor, but death we have been doomed to. Not to receive honour were we summoned, but to be branded with infamy. Grant your soldiers this boon: Sacrifice us for Christ, and kill us for His sake, whose empire alone we acknowledge. Pay fire with fire, and for the ashes of that sacrifice burn us to ashes. Cut off our hands, those hands we did wickedly stretch forth, and our feet that carried to an evil deed. Let others have your gifts, who need not be shamed to take them; for us Christ is enough and more than enough, whom we value above all price.'

"Such the language they held, and at the same time aroused their fellows to realise the cheat, and recover from their intoxication and appease Christ with their blood. Then was the Emperor greatly angered; yet would he not kill them openly, that they might not be made martyrs, which were martyrs already so far as in them lay, but punished them with exile and avenged the slight done him by this penalty. But herein did he only benefit them exceedingly, by removing of them far from his odious sacrifices and malicious designs."

Thus the most blessed Nazianzen, showing us beyond a doubt how these most gallant champions of Christ could neither by the scorn nor the cunning of that most wicked and apostate Emperor be cast down from the height of their piety, but were thereby but rendered more steadfast and ready to endure death for Christ's sake. Thus was Julian's cunning all in vain, and his attempt to turn them from the faith of Christ brought to naught.

TWO OTHER LIKE DEVICES, WHEREBY THE HEATHEN THOUGHT THEY
COULD CAJOLE THE CHRISTIANS TO FORSWEAR THEIR FAITH.

Eusebius doth relate in his *Ecclesiastical History* how
Christians were sometimes, under the Emperor Diocletian,
forced to join the number of those sacrificing, so as to appear
to have made offering to idols. This is what he saith : " Now
of the remainder each did endure one or other of divers forms
of torment ; one had all his body torn with whips, another
suffered the racking of all his limbs, another was mangled
with sharp razors beyond all human endurance. Amongst
whom were some which scarce made an altogether honourable
end, and some that endured the trial to little purpose. For
there were unfaithful servants ; and while one would be
violently shoved forward and brought up to perform these
foul and abominable rites, and then, albeit he had never
sacrificed at all, yet would be let go just as if he had duly
made offering ; another, though he had never been near the
Temple or touched aught impure, yet in virtue of his heathen
friends certifying he had sacrificed, would so bear their scorn
in silence and save himself from the peril. One, rescued
half dead and half alive, is cast forth as a dead man ; another,
prostrated on the earth and counted in the number of worshippers, is dragged away stealthily by the feet till out of all
danger. On the contrary some cried out and announced in
a loud voice, how they utterly and entirely disavowed the very
ceremony they were taking part in ; others boasting and
openly confessing the life-giving name of Christ, proclaimed

themselves Christians; while others again declared emphatically they had never offered sacrifice to idols and never would. Nevertheless, even these, struck in the mouth and forced to silence, battered and buffeted on face and cheeks by the rough hands of numerous attendants appointed for the purpose, were at last violently expelled the assemblage, and so deemed it a great thing gained, that albeit really enemies of righteousness, they yet had the appearance of having completely accomplished what they had it in their minds to do."

The same pretence again was practised by these servants of Satan in yet another way; for they were used to put the meat offered to idols into the Christians' mouths against their will, and to pour the wine of sacrifice down their throats. So in the *Acts* of the Blessed Martyrs, Saints Tharacus, Probus, and Andronicus, are handed down to everlasting memory certain noble words of these holy men: "After this, the Governor ordered flesh which had been offered and wine of sacrifice to be brought, and said, 'Pour the wine down his throat and put meat from the altar into his mouth.' And whilst this was being done, Probus cried, 'May the Lord look down from His seat on high and see the compulsion used, and judge my case justly.' The Governor said, 'Many torments have you endured, unhappy man; and now you have accepted the sacrifice.' Probus replied, 'Little have you effected, by using compulsion; the Lord knoweth my true heart.' The Governor cried, 'Nay! but you have both eaten and drunk.' Probus answered, 'The Lord knoweth and hath seen the compulsion I am under.'" And again a little further on, the same author, speaking of St. Andronicus: "The Governor said, 'Open his lips, and put in his mouth flesh from the altar, and pour the wine down his throat.' Whilst this was being done, Andronicus exclaimed, 'Lord, Lord! I suffer compulsion.' The Governor asked, 'How long can you endure under torture? There! you have tasted of the sacrifice.' Andronicus made answer, 'All men are sinners which worship idols, you and your Emperors alike.'"

But to return from a digression which hath been longer than our intention was, let us now proceed to other matters still remaining to be expounded, to wit the fashions, which were many and divers, wherein the Holy Martyrs were given to the fire. Sometimes were they bound to upright stakes, and a fire kindled round them, or stretched out and tied to four pegs and a blaze made underneath; sometimes were they cast into fiery furnaces, into a flaming pile, or into pits full of live coals, or else thrown into great tuns or casks. Sometimes, again, they were consumed in chambers, shrines, or baths, wherein they were imprisoned by their heathen persecutors, and which were set on fire and burned with the martyrs inside; at others tied with ropes of flax saturated with oil, their bodies drenched with sulphur and resin, their feet bound about with flax dipped in oil, and then set alight, or else set in boats filled with tow and pitch, and then fired so as to be burned at sea, did they holily and happily render back their unpolluted and unstained soul to God, the Maker and Creator of all things.

FIG. XXVII.

Martyrs sent to sea in a ship filled with combustibles and set on fire.

*To face p.* 150

150a

All these things be attested in the *Acts* of divers Martyrs—
the first fashion of death (bound to stakes and so burned) in
the *Histories* of St. Polycarp and St. Tharacus; the second
(tied to four pegs and a fire kindled beneath) in the *Acts* of
St. Anastasia, a Roman virgin and martyr; the third, fourth,
fifth, and sixth (thrown into furnaces, pits, or casks to be
burned) in the *Acts* of Saints Emilianus and Paphnutius, of
three sisters, Faith, Hope, and Charity, virgins and martyrs,
of Saints Agnes, Apollonia, and Dorothy, virgins and martyrs
likewise. In the history of the last named, St. Dorothy, we do
read how two sisters, Christé and Calisté, were brought back by
her holy care to the fold of the Christian Faith, from the which
they had fallen away, in these words : "The Governor sent a
message to Christé and Calisté, bidding them to his presence
along with Dorothy; and after taking them on one side, he
began to ask them whether they had succeeded in changing
Dorothy's sentiments. But with one voice they made answer :
'We were mistaken and did act very sinfully, when through
fear of punishment and momentary pain we did sacrifice to
idols, and asked her to do the like; but she led us to re-
pentance, so that we may now win Christ's mercy.' Then
Sapritius (for such was the Governor's name) tears his
clothes, and with exceeding fury ordered them to be tied
together back to back and so cast into a tun or cask, an if
they would not do sacrifice. . . ."

Of the seventh sort — being imprisoned in chambers,
shrines, or baths, and there burned or suffocated — we find
record in the *Acts* of Saints Domna and Theophila, virgins

and martyrs, and of the Roman virgins and holy martyrs, Flavia Domitilla, Theodora, Euphrosyné and Cæcilia.

WHAT WAS MEANT BY SUFFOCATION IN AN OVER-HEATED BATH.

We read in the *History* of St. Cæcilia, how that she was shut up and stifled in a hot bath. It should be understood therefore that this was likewise a custom sometimes observed among the Ancients, to put to death criminals and offenders or Christians in the baths. At times they were used to imprison such in the first or hottest chamber of the baths, the same which was called the Sweating Room or *Laconicum*, that stifled therein by the excessive heat, they might give up life for death. Now the ancient Thermæ, or Hot Baths, did consist of four Chambers, whereof the first, used for provoking sweat, was called the Sweating Room, or *Laconicum*, or Hot Room for Copious Sweating; the other three being the Hot, the Tepid, and the Cooling Room, respectively.

In the first room or *Laconicum* (as explained above), the Blessed Martyrs were sometimes done to death. So in the *History* of St. Cæcilia you will find it writ : "Then being exceeding wroth, Almachius the Judge commanded her to be taken back to her own house, and there consumed by the heat of the Baths. But albeit she was shut up in the hot air of her bath-house and great store of wood supplied thereunder day and night, yet did she remain unharmed therein, as if placed only in the Cold Chamber, and perfectly safe through God's grace, in such wise that no least part of all her limbs was wet with so much as the smallest trace of sweat."

From this we see it was the *Laconicum* or Hot Chamber wherein they were shut up which were killed in the Baths. So Gallenus, writing of the *Laconicum*, saith : "On entering, they tarry in the hot air, that is in the *Laconicum;* later on, they go down into a bath of hot water." We gather moreover from the *Acts* of the same Saint Cæcilia that this *Laconicum* was employed for inflicting death on offenders, by imprisoning folk therein, men or women, and so keeping them shut up while great quantities of fuel were continuously piled up and consumed underneath.

But we must now go on to consider the remaining fashions wherein Christians were burned with fire by the Heathen, to wit the eighth, ninth, and tenth modes—tied with ropes saturated in oil, feet bound with flax dipped in oil, bound and sent to sea in boats loaded with tow and pitch and set alight. Of all these we have sure witness in divers *Acts* of the Saints,—of the last named in the *History* of St. Restituta, virgin and martyr, of the eighth and ninth in the accounts of the passion of St. Amphianus and of St. Ursicius. The former is recorded in the *Roman Martyrology* under April 2 in these words, "At Cæsarea in Palestine, anniversary of St. Amphianus the Martyr, who in the Persecution of Maximin, for having remonstrated with Urbanus the Governor for sacrificing to idols, was cruelly scourged, and most bitterly tortured, his feet being wrapped in flax dipped in oil and then set on fire, and finally thrown into the sea. So passing through fire and water, he was brought at last to blissful consolation." The other, St. Ursicius, is commemorated in the Greek *Menology* under August 24 : "Commemoration of the Blessed Martyr St. Ursicius, who under the Emperor Maximin was denounced to the Emperor from the city of Sibentum, lying inland from Illyricum, and handed over to the Governor Aristides. When he remained steadfast and unwavering in his profession, he was first violently scourged with bulls' pizzles, then bound round with ropes of flax steeped in oil, and himself drenched with sulphur and resin, he was set alight ; last of all sentence of death was pronounced, and the Holy St. Ursicius was slain with a drawn sword by the informer Valens. And having so won martyrdom, he was given to the tomb by a pious woman, Simplicia by name."

OF THE DEADLY TUNIC AS AN INSTRUMENT OF MARTYRDOM.

These forms of torture, whereby the most glorious Martyrs Amphianus and Ursicius died, are very like, if indeed we may not call them the same, as a most terrible punishment which the Ancients called the *Deadly Tunic*. This was a shirt smeared and saturated with inflammatory substances (as Seneca, *Epistles*, records), which, being presently set alight, did burn up in a fearful conflagration the criminals wrapped in it, such as had been convicted of some more than usually grave offence. Both Tertullian and Cælius make mention of this punishment as applied to Christian martyrs.

Tortures of a like kind to this were those inflicted by the Heretics of our own day, as recorded in the *Theatre of Cruelties*, on Domitius Hurley, which had been created by Pope Gregory, thirteenth of the name, by reason of his

FIG. XXVIII.

A. Martyr cast into a burning fiery furnace.
B. Martyrs set in a tun, or cask, and burned therein.
C. Martyr burned in a room, or chamber, that hath been set on fire.
D. Bound hand and foot and set on a blazing pile.

E. Bound to four pegs fixed in the ground, with a fire burning underneath.
F. Bound with ropes drenched in oil and consumed by a fire lighted under him.
G. Thrown into a pit full of live coals.
H. Iron shovel for stirring and rousing the fire.

154a

To face p. 154

singular and pre-eminent piety and excellence of life, Arch-
bishop of Cashel in Ireland, his native country. Accused of
the offence of having fortified some children with the Holy
Sacrament of Confirmation, he was arrested; and forasmuch
as he refused to renounce the Catholic faith, he was subjected
by the fury of the Heretics to the tortures of the question.
For greaves or leggings filled full of oil were put upon his
legs, and then tied fast on a wooden seat so that he could not
move, he was set before a huge fire, and the leggings being
burnt up by the fierce flame, his shins were consumed along
with them, in such wise that when the heretics came to draw
off the leggings, they tore away the flesh with them up to his
knees, leaving only the bare bones. One morning soon after
this, about three or four of the clock, his neck was set in a
noose of osiers, that his agony might be the longer, and he
was so hanged. Thus did he win the noble crown of martyrdom, and his spirit took flight to the skies."

However, seeing that in connection with the *Deadly Tunic*
we have spoken of the Catholics being tortured by fire at the
hands of the Heretics of our own time, that we may not in any
wise appear to slight the martyrs of Orthodoxy which were
punished by fire in divers ways by the more ancient Heretics
under those most wicked Emperors, Constantius, Valens, Leo
the Isaurian and Constantine Copronymus, as well as under
the Arian Vandals, we will quote some instances from the
Holy Fathers or from the *Histories* of their lives. And first
concerning the Catholics which were tormented by fire under
Constantius, this is what St. Athanasius saith, " But all these

(that is the Arians, enemies of the Orthodox Church) they did shun as murderers, malefactors and robbers, forasmuch as they overthrew Monasteries and set fire to the same for to burn the Monks, and tore down their dwelling places . . . ," and again in his *Apology*, " For setting virgins on blazing fires, they strove thus to force them to confess the Arian faith. Further details of the Catholics similarly persecuted under Valens are found in the *History* of Theodoretus, " But at Constantinople the Arians did load a ship with a company of pious priests, and launch the same into the deep without sails or tackle. Then embarking sundry adherents of their own sect in another vessel, they bid them set on fire the ship containing the priests. So this being done, the priests, after struggling a while with fire and sea, are presently plunged in the deep, and so win the crown of martyrdom." Similar accounts you may find in Sozomen and Socrates in their *Ecclesiastical Histories;* as also in Victor concerning the Catholics under the Vandal Persecution, "Some they slew by scourging, some by hanging, others they burned in bonfires," and again, writing of the martyrdom of St. Liberatus and his companions, " This, however, came to the Tyrant's ears, who, intoxicated with fury, orders them to be subjected to tortures hitherto unheard of and to be laden with heavier chains. Moreover he commands a ship to be filled with bundles of dry faggots, and all his victims being bound fast therein, to be set alight on the open sea and burned up. . . ."

Lastly concerning the Orthodox which were martyred under Leo or Constantine Copronymus, the *Roman Martyr-*

ology hath the following under August 29, "Anniversary of Saints Hypatius and Andrew. These were two priests which for the respect they showed the sacred images were slaughtered by Leo, after their beards had been steeped in pitch and set alight, and the scalp of their heads torn off." The same is related under November 28 of St. Stephen the Younger, who is said to have endured the like punishment under Constantine Copronymus.

CHAPTER IX

Of other Instruments of Torture and Modes employed for the tormenting of Christian Martyrs, such as Schoolboys' Iron Styles, Nails, Saws, Spears, Swords and Arrows, Tearing out the Inwards, Cutting the Throat, Beheading, Branding and Marking, Pounding with Axes and Clubs

STILL vehemently desiring to make prey of the souls of men, each and all, the Devil did never cease industriously to seek other modes and manners whereby he might utterly overthrow and drive out the Faith of Christ. So, deeming he had won a means of easily accomplishing his fell purpose, to wit persisting alway in his savage practices against Christ's members, he did cause all the great judges of those times to opine that this and this alone would make their wisdom renowned, if they aye ordered such men and women as were champions and heralds of our Religion to be most cruelly tortured, tormented and put to death with every agony of pain that could possibly be devised. Oh, shallow ingenuity! idle thought! Verily, verily, were these wise men made foolish, their cunning devices and evil counsels brought to naught!

"For indeed,"—as Eusebius saith in his *Ecclesiastical History*,—"the hands of the executioners failed, and albeit succeeding one another in relays, the men were wearied out, and the edge of their sword blunted. Myself saw the tormentors sit back exhausted, recover strength, regain breath, take fresh swords,—and yet the day not be long enough for all the torments to be inflicted! Nevertheless, not one of all the band, not so much as one child of tender years, could be frightened back from affronting death; the one and only thing each dreaded was, that when the hurrying sun ended the short day, he should be left behind, divided from the society of his martyred comrades. Thus did they, one and all, steadfastly and boldly trusting to the Faith, welcome with joy and exultation a present death as the beginning of eternal life. In a word, while the first batches were being slaughtered, the rest would stand singing psalms and hymns to God, each waiting his own turn of martyrdom, that so they might breathe forth their last breath in praises to the Almighty."

Mighty the failure of these servants of Satan, and great their foolishness! Verily did they tumble into the pit they had digged for the Saints to fall into! Again and again did they condemn,—but all in vain,—their Christian adversaries to be torn limb from limb, to be stabbed to death with countless blows of iron writing styles or, what is the same thing, schoolboys' pens, to be stuck over with nails, either their whole body or some special part of it, to be cut in half with saws, to be transfixed with spears, to be pierced with swords, to be shot with arrows; their bellies to be gashed open

and the inwards torn out, their throats to be cut ; to be
beheaded, to be disfigured with brands and markings ; their
heads to be pounded with axes or clubs, and dashed to pieces ;
women's bosoms to be amputated, and their tongues, hands,
and feet, as well as men's, to be cut away ; their legs to be
broken, their teeth pulled out, their skin cruelly flayed from
their living bodies, their bodies impaled with a sharp stake ;
nails, eyes, and face to be tortured with keen-pointed reeds ;
to be hurled headlong from high places, to be dragged over
ground sown with thorns and thistles and thickly covered with
sharp stones by untamed horses or in other ways, to be
exposed to wild beasts, to be buried alive in the earth, to
be cast into a running river, thrown into a limekiln, stripped
naked and led through the public streets. Or else, whenever
two trees could be found growing near together, a branch
of each being bent down so as to meet, to either of these one
of the martyr's feet was tied in such a way that the boughs
which had been forcibly drawn together, when let go, returned with a bound to their natural position and, tearing the
man's body in two which was fastened to them, rent his limbs
asunder and bare them back with them. Or lastly, these idol
worshippers would give judgment for the Christians to be
driven into exile, utterly deprived of every solace, or sent
forth to cut blocks of marble, dig sand and carry the same on
their own shoulders to their edifices which were then a-building,
or else to be deported to the mines. With such torments, and
others described in former chapters, yea ! and others again,
the names whereof for their exceeding cruelty Eusebius doth

confess himself ignorant of,—with all these were Christ's most
blessed soldiers tortured. Yet could they never be vanquished
by any of them; but guarded by the protection of heaven,
they did suffer and endure every anguish bravely and steadfastly. "For truly they stood forth" (to use St. Ephraem's
words) "in the time of trial most gallant warriors of God,
bearing every torment with the utmost readiness in the name
of the only-begotten Son of God, our Saviour Jesus Christ.
How strong were they and what a glory of gallant endurance
they acquired, who, seeing all the horrid preparations of
torture then before their eyes, not only felt no fear, but contending with all the greater constancy, overcame all suffering
by their steadfastness! They looked on the blazing pile, and
red-hot pans, and boiling caldrons, which in their fierce
ebullition shot out afar drops of pitch and melted fat.
They gazed upon the wheels, iron-shod and iron-spiked,
turning with fierce velocity amid the flames. They beheld
the iron claws and glowing plates, the cudgels, the bears and
lions, precipices, handspikes, augers, fetters and chains, in a
word all the devices the Arch-Enemy of Truth hath invented
against the holy confessors of the Lord and Saviour. For
every sort of torment was spread by the wily foe in sight
of the martyrs to make the Saints afraid, that their tongues,
struck dumb by the mere sight of such horrors, might no more
dare to confess the Lord Jesus. But what effect on these
faithful and eager warriors of Christ had this exhibition of
horrible and unheard of tortures? Why! to make them more
eager yet, with greater confidence and increased firmness,

M

unhesitatingly and intrepidly to confess their Saviour Christ before the tribunals of Judges and Administrators! Neither crackling flames, nor fiery pans, nor boiling pots, nor hurtling wheels, nor red-hot plates, nor toothed claws and other the like instruments, nor fetters and ponderous chains, nor tyrants' menaces, nor Princes' threats, nor all the Devil's and his servants' wiles, availed to terrify Christ's intrepid soldiers, or force them to abjure their faith or withdraw from the allegiance of their God and Saviour. Rather, girt about with faith, they trod underfoot all the machinations of the Evil One, and consternation gat no hold upon them.

"Hast seen the strength of Christ's faithful followers? hast seen the glory of the soldiers of the Saviour, and their steadfastness? hast seen the wondrous alacrity of them that seek the kingdom of heaven with all their heart, and love Christ their king with all their might? hast seen the perfect faith of them that have been truly made perfect? hast seen the charity that burns in the holy bosoms of martyrs, for the which they have scorned all earthly joys, to hold to their God whom they have chosen? hast seen Christ's loving-kindness, whereby He raiseth heavenward them that desire to be exalted aloft? hast seen triumphant Paradise embrace and cherish Christ's champions which were eager for its bliss, now rejoicing in eternal light and peace? Come hither, dearest reader, and consider and contemplate the glorious triumphs of the martyrs; behold with the eyes of the heart the abounding faith of these heavenly strivers, and the inviolable ardour of their piety. No weight of agony could move these just men's resolution;

Fig. XXIX.

A. Martyr stabbed to death by boys with their writing styles.

B. Martyr whose limbs are amputated one by one.

To face p. 162

not death itself extinguish the zeal of their undaunted love. Beaten, they welcomed with a great joy the blows of the rods as the keenest of delights ; with calm and smiling faces they rendered thanks to God, for that they had been deemed worthy to suffer for His sake."

So far St. Ephraem. But to return from this digression, we must now expound each of these several sorts of tortures above named and confirm the same from the *Histories* of the Blessed Martyrs. The first—martyrs torn limb from limb—is attested by the *Acts* of St. Nicephorus, commemorated in the *Roman Martyrology* under February 25, and of St. James, surnamed *Intercisus* ("cut in pieces") ; the second by St. Gregory Nazianzen, Victor, *On the Vandal Persecution*, as likewise the *History* of the martyrdom of St. Cassianus.

IRON WRITING STYLES OR BOYS' PENS,—WHAT THEY ARE, AND TO WHAT PURPOSES THEY WERE TURNED.

This was an instrument of brass, wherewith writing was executed in Ancient times on a white ground, that is on waxed tablets, just as our merchants are used to write now-adays on wooden memorandum books or billets. So in chapter xix. of the Book of Job, "Oh that my words were now written ! Oh that they were inscribed in a book ! that with an iron pen and lead they were graven. . . ." Likewise Plautus, *Bacchides* :—

> . . . *Affer cito.*
> *Quid ? Stylum, ceram, tabellas et linum*

and again :—

Habes tabellas ?   Vis rogare ?
Habeo stylum

(". . . Bring quickly.   What ?   Your style, wax, tablets and thread," *i.e.* the thread with which the tablets were tied together when sent as a letter.—"Have you your tablets ? Can you ask ?   I have my style too.")

Accordingly with these writing styles, as a very painful form of death, those condemned to die were often stabbed.   This is attested by many authors, and these the most trustworthy, as by Suetonius, *Life of the Emperor Caius*, in these words : "Wishing the Senator's destruction, he suborned men to assail him as he left the Senate House, and suddenly inveighing against him as a public enemy, to stab him with their writing pens and pass him on to others to be yet further mangled."   Also Seneca, "Erixio, a Roman Knight, was within our own memory stabbed to death by the populace in the Forum with their writing pens, because he had killed his son by flogging."   The same likewise is witnessed by the *Acts* of St. Mark of Arethusa, where we read, "From one crowd of boys to another was Mark tossed, swinging to and fro, as they caught that noble body on their sharp pens or styles ;" likewise the *Acts* of St. Cassian the Martyr, "Hereupon the holy man was questioned by the persecutor and asked what knowledge or special skill he had that he must teach the boys their letters ; to which he answered, etc. . . . ;" and a little lower down, "Then stripped of his clothes, and with hands tied behind him, he is made to stand up in the midst; and the lads being called in by teaching whom he had become odious, they were given leave to do him to death. So they, learning what injury they had received, and burning to revenge themselves accordingly, proceeded some to batter him with their tablets, others to strike him with their writing styles. And in this scene of martyrdom the weaker the hands engaged, the heavier was the pain of the victim, as death was the more protracted."

But it was two different things to be tormented with goads and to be stabbed with iron styles. With the former offenders were merely tortured, but with the latter both tortured and most cruelly done to death. Moreover, the former, which is known as goading, was used to be applied merely to slaves that had been guilty of stealing, the latter was inflicted on prisoners convicted of the gravest crimes. The former mode of punishment is spoken of by Prudentius in his *Hymn* of the Martyr St. Hippolytus :—

Iliaque infestis perfodiunt stimulis

("And they stab his sides with painful goads"); also repeatedly by Plautus, for instance in the *Asinaria* :—

Utinam nunc mihi stimulus in manu sit,

and in the *Menoechmi* :—

At ego te pendentem fodiam stimulis triginta dies

("Would I had my goad in my hand this minute;" "But I will hang you up and dig you with the goads for thirty days"); to which we may add a line from the same play of the *Menoechmi* as a further illustration :—

Jam ascendo in currum, jam lora teneo, jam stimulus in manu est

("Now I mount the chariot, now I grasp the reins, now the goad is in my hands"). All these passages serve to show the goad was a rod or reed with a sharp point such as rustics use to prod up oxen with, and this is confirmed by the *Acts* of St. Joseph the Martyr, where we find it writ, "But tying a point to a long reed, they ordered the Saint to be pricked therewith."—But enough of this part of our subject.

To come to the third and fourth kinds of torture, wherein the Holy Martyrs were stuck over with nails or cut in two with iron saws, these are shown forth in the *Acts* of Saints Paphnutius (*Roman Martyrology*, September 24), and Severus, Bishop (*ib.*, November 7), Saints Fausta and Euphemia, virgins and martyrs, and others besides. The second of these punishments, the fourth to wit, that of sawing asunder, is recorded likewise by Suetonius, *Life of the Emperor Caius,* where he speaks of certain persons condemned on accusation to this doom. Of this form of torture we shall speak again further on; it had the effect of branding the name of the Emperor Caligula (Caius) with a reputation of cruelty for all ages. All this should teach us the lesson how fierce was the rage of the Heathen against Christ's soldiers, and how steadfast on the other hand the constancy and valour of Christian men, whereby they did easily and unconcernedly suffer and overcome every sort and description of torment.

The fifth kind of torture, wherein Christians were pierced with augers or gimlets, is attested by the *Acts* of the holy Virgins and Martyred Saints, Faith, Hope, and Charity, three sisters already spoke of on an earlier page, as also in the

FIG. XXX.

A. Martyr stabbed in the throat with a dagger.
B. Shot to death with arrows.
C. Beaten over the head with an axe

D. Beheaded with a sword.
E. Transfixed with a spear.

To face p. 166

account of St. Fausta, a virgin martyr commemorated in the *Roman Martyrology*, under September 20 : "At Cyzicus in the Propontis, anniversary of the Blessed Martyrs, Fausta, a virgin, and Eulasius, slain under the Emperor Maximian. Of these twain, Fausta was made bald by this same Eulasius, which was priest of the idols, and her head shaven in scorn, then hung up and tortured. When finally he was for cutting her in two, but the executioners could do her no hurt, Eulasius was astounded and believed on Christ. So whilst he in his turn was being violently tortured by the Emperor's orders, Fausta was pierced with an auger in the head, stuck all over with nails, and finally set in a frying-pan over the fire, and so with the other, summoned by a voice from heaven, ascended to the Lord."

The sixth kind, whereby Christians were transfixed with spears or swords, may be illustrated from the *Histories* of Saints Marcus and Marcellianus, Saints Benignus and Cyril, the latter a deacon, Saints Fusca, Basilla, Anatholia and Justina, virgins and martyrs, and of St. Polycarp.

To go on to the seventh, the tearing open of the sufferers' bellies, this cruelty is attested in the *History* of St. Cyril, whose martyrdom is recorded in the *Roman Martyrology* under March 26 in these words, "At Heliopolis in the Lebanon region, anniversary of St. Cyril, deacon and martyr, whose belly was cut open and his liver torn out, whereon the Heathen did foully feast. This was done under the Emperor Julian,— the Apostate." The same is related in the *Acts* of St. Eucratis or Eugratia, virgin and martyr, concerning whose death the

following is found writ in the *Martyrology* under April 16,
" At Cæsaraugusta (Saragossa) in Spain, anniversary of Saint
Eucratis, virgin and martyr, who after her body had been
mangled, her breast cut off and her liver torn out, was shut up
still alive in gaol till her body did rot away and mortify."

OF OTHER TORMENTS AND TORTURES, BOTH SIMILAR TO THE FOREGOING AND EKE DIVERS, TO THE WHICH CHRISTIAN VIRGINS WERE SUBJECTED.

It was first under the rule of the Emperor Julian, surnamed
the Apostate, that holy virgins were torn open. Then, whilst
their bellies were yet quivering and heaving, they were stuffed
with barley and exposed to be devoured by wild hogs. This
is recorded in each and every detail by St. Gregory Nazianzen,
who writes, "For they (the men of Heliopolis),—to relate only
one actrocity out of many, but one that may well rouse the
horror even of godless Heathens,—are said to have taken
chaste virgins, superior to the world's attractions and which
had scarce ever yet so much as been seen of men, and setting
them in a public place, to have stripped them naked, that they
might first shame them by exposing them to the general gaze.
Afterward tearing and cutting open their bellies (Oh, Christ !
how imitate Thy patient long-suffering at that time ?), they did
first chew their flesh with their own teeth and swallow the same,
and, as was agreeable to their abominable fury, did gorge
themselves on their raw livers, and having once tasted such
food, made it their common and usual diet ; then secondly,
while the inwards were yet quivering, they stuffed in pigs' food,

and letting in wild hogs, offered the horrid spectacle for folk to see of the girls' flesh being mangled and eaten together with the barley. . . ."

All this shows us that these Christian virgins were treated in this horrible way by way of ignominy,—the same reason for which they were stripped of their clothes, for no greater shame can be inflicted on maidens than to be seen naked by lustful and wanton eyes.

Shame of this sort was inflicted on those Holy Virgins of Christ, Saints Prisca, Agnes, Barbara, Christina, Euphemia of Aquileia and her three sisters, to wit Dorothy, Thecla, and Erasma, and many others to boot. Beside which, many and sundry other ways of shaming and insulting holy virgins were resorted to. For instance, their hair was shaved off, as is related in the *Histories* of the blessed Saints Fausta, Charitina, Christina, and other virgin martyrs. And to see how shameful an insult it was to women to shave their heads, read the *Acts* of the Saints just quoted, Suetonius, *Life of Caius Caligula,* and especially what is writ in the *Roman Martyrology* concerning St. Fausta, who, as therein recorded, was shaven by way of insult.

Moreover, with a like purpose of shame and ignominy, Christian maidens, to the insulting of our holy Faith, were given over to panders or to wanton youths, or taken to public brothels to have their maidenhood violated there. Yet God, by whose nod all things are ruled, willed their virtue to be saved and themselves offered to him an unstained sacrifice.

If the question be asked why these atrocities were perpetrated by wicked men on virgins dedicate to Christ, we may answer as above that this was done by way of insult to the Christian religion. Yet another motive may likewise be alleged, the fact that by old-established custom of the Romans (so saith Suetonius in his *Life of Tiberius*) it was unlawful for a virgin to be violently put to death, except first she had been deflowered by her executioners or by whore-mongers. I will quote the Historian's actual words, "Unripe girls, forasmuch as by established custom it was forbid that virgins be strangled, these were first violated by the hangman and then executed."

From this you may readily learn, unless you are wilfully blind, the goodness and the power of Christ, who knoweth how to safeguard his brides when so exposed to peril and danger and preserve their virtue intact, reserving and liberating them from the hands of insolent and unruly men. This is proved by Basil the Great, who saith in his book *On True Virginity*, "When the fierceness of persecution was at its height, the virgins which were chosen out for their faithful love of the Bridegroom and delivered up to the mockery of impious men, remained unsullied in their bodies, forasmuch as He for whose sake they bare these things rendered vain the assaults of sinners upon their flesh, and kept their bodies unsoiled by the miracle of His divine power." The same is attested by the *Acts* of the Blessed Saints and Virgins, Agnes, Daria, Seraphia, Theodora, Lucy, Susanna, and many others.—But enough said of these tortures and torments, wherewith Christian virgins were afflicted at the hands of heathen persecutors.

The Heretics likewise under the Emperors Constantius, son
of Constantine the Great, and Valens, and during the most
savage persecution of the Catholics by the Vandals, afflicted
with like insults and ignominies of divers sorts the holy and
virgin brides of Christ. Of such abominations under Constantius we are told by St. Athanasius (*Apology*) in these
words : "Now virgins were set in the flames of a blazing pile
by that most abandoned of mankind Sebastianus, leader of the
troops, to force them to declare for the Arian doctrine. Then
when he found them steadfast against this torture, he strips
them naked and beats them so sorely on the face, that for long
after their friends could scarce recognise them," and in another
place, "The Arians whip and scourge the sacred bodies of
virgins, and putting rude hands beneath their clothes drag
them along, and bare their heads, nay! when they resisted
and would not come, cuff and kick them. Cruel treatment
this, but more cruel yet followed,—treatment altogether in-
tolerable by reason of its shameful indecency. For knowing
the maidens' shamefacedness and innocency of evil words, and
how they could more readily endure stoning and cudgelling
than foul speeches, they would accompany their violence with
the most abominable expressions, and prompt to similar
language the younger men which were prone to ribald laughter
at such evil words and evil deeds. But the holy virgins and
other pure-minded women would recoil from such talk as from
the bite of serpents. Moreover, the open enemies of Christ
likewise added their help to the perpetration of these horrors,
and it is no falsehood to say, chimed in with the others in their

filthy utterances, for they undoubtedly took a delight in the foulness of the talk the young men indulged in ; " and yet again further on, "Many virgins which were for rebuking their impiety and speaking up for the truth, they drave out of their houses ; others they insulted as they went about their business, and had them stripped by the more wanton and disorderly youths, and gave their own women leave to treat them with whatever indignities they would."

Of like indignities shown to holy virgins under the same Emperor the Historian Theodoretus doth also speak : "George the Arian compelled virgins which had vowed themselves to lifelong chastity not only to deny the confession of St. Athanasius, but to pronounce accursed the faith of their fathers. His associate and confederate in these cruelties was a certain Sebastian, Prefect of the Troops, who, kindling a pile in the middle of the city, and making the virgins to stand naked beside it, bade them abjure their religion. But being so set, a sad and a bitter sight for believers and unbelievers alike, yet held they this ignominy as the greatest honour."

Of virgins similarly mocked and scorned under the Emperor Valens, Peter of Alexander writes, quoted in the *History* of Theodoretus, "Palladius entering the Catholics' Church, begins with his forces, instead of solemn words such as were befitting the place, to sing burlesque litanies to the holy images ; instead of reading the divine Scriptures to utter unseemly shouts. They feared not to indulge in dissolute words and obscene language and to pour insults upon the virgins of Christ. . . . And would that they had remained

Fig. XXXI.

A. Martyr tortured with an auger.   C. Pierced with nails.
B. Stabbed with a dagger.

To face p. 172

content with foul words, sinning only in them, and not far surpassed the abomination of their language by the atrocity of their deeds! For abuse, however violent, is yet to be borne, especially of them whose minds are filled with the prudence and divine teaching of Christ. But these men, vessels of wrath doomed to destruction, making a loud and wanton noise that burst from their great noses like water, so to speak, from an aqueduct, began to tear the dresses of Christ's virgins, whose holy life made them an ensample to godly folk, and to lead them about naked as they were born in triumph up and down the city, and in their wantonness to mock the same insolently and indecently, perpetrating deeds that were at once cruel and barbarous. But an if anyone was moved to pity and tried either to stay them by force or dissuade them by words from such abominations, he did not escape without wounds. Alas! many maidens were forcibly violated, and many struck over the head with clubs, were left lying speechless. Nor was leave given to commit their bodies to the tomb; indeed in many cases these were sought for in vain by their parents with much weeping, but never found."

Lastly concerning virgins which were ignominiously handled under the Arian Vandals to the contempt of the true Church of Christ, Victor, Bishop of Utica, thus bears witness, "Then the Tyrant ordered the consecrated virgins to be assembled together, urging the Vandals, with midwives of their own race, to inspect and scrutinise, contrary to the laws of modesty, the shamefaced secrets of their privy parts, when neither their mothers were present nor any of the matrons.

Then hanging the girls up cruelly, and cruelly burning them, fastening great weights to their feet, they afterward applied red-hot plates of iron to back, belly, breasts, and sides. Moreover they were asked in the intervals of torture, 'Tell us now how the Bishops lie with you, and your Priests.' And by this cruelty of torment we know that very many were killed there and then, while the others which were left alive were crippled and bent double by the drying up and contraction of the skin."

All this doth plainly and abundantly inform us that the Heretics of former days (whose evil ensample more recent Heretics do follow, as we learn from many authorities) did prove themselves, in venting their hatred of the Catholic religion on the holy virgins, and heaping insult upon the same, without a doubt more inhuman, more wanton, more merciless, and more cruel than the Heathen.

But to leave the Heretics for the present, we must proceed to the exposition of the eighth kind of torture among those named at the beginning of the chapter. This torment, the shooting of Christians with arrows, is attested by the *Histories* of many martyrs, particularly of the two hundred and sixty, whose names are unknown to us, but who are recorded by the *Roman Martyrology*, under March 1, as having so died ; likewise of St. Martha and her sons, Saints Irenis and Christina, virgins and martyrs, Saints Sebastian, Christopher and Faustus, of which last record is given in the Greek *Menology*, under July 16, in the following words, "Same day, anniversary of the Blessed Martyr, St. Faustus, which under the Emperor

Decius, by reason of his confession of the Christian Faith, was arrested, and freely professing himself a servant of Christ, was fixed to a cross and wounded with arrows. After remaining five whole days on the cross without flinching, he did at last commend his spirit into the hands of God. Again many Catholics are recorded by Victor (*Vandal Persecution*) to have been shot to death. He writes, "On one occasion the Eastertide rites were being celebrated, and our people having met in a place called the Palace to honour Easter Day, and shut and locked the Church upon themselves, the Arians discovered this. Immediately one of the priests, Andiot by name, collecting together a band of armed men, started to attack the company of innocent worshippers. They rush up with drawn swords, seize other arms, and some of them, climbing on to the roofs, shoot showers of arrows through the windows of the Church. Just then, as it befell, God's people were singing, and a reader was standing up in the pulpit intoning the hallelujah versicle. At that moment an arrow caught him in the throat, and the book falling from his hand, he, too, fell down dead. Many others likewise are known to have been killed by arrows and darts in the very middle of the platform of the Altar. . . ."

The ninth mode of torture,—that wherein the martyrs' throats were cut,—is attested in the *History* of St. Philip and his daughter St. Eugenia, a Roman virgin and martyr, as likewise in the account of the death of Saints Justus and Pastor, two brothers, given in the *Roman Martyrology* under August 13 : "In Spain, anniversary of the Blessed Martyrs,

Saints Justus and Pastor, brothers. When already well advanced in letters, they threw down their writing-tablets in the school, and of their own free impulse ran forth to meet martyrdom. Soon they were ordered by Dacian, the Governor of the Province, to be arrested and beaten with clubs; and after gallantly strengthening one another's constancy with mutual appeals, were led forth of the city, and their throats were cut by the public executioner."

Of the tenth sort, where martyrs were condemned to be beheaded, witness is afforded by well-nigh countless *Histories* of the Blessed Martyrs,—notably of Saints Terence, Pompey, and their companions, Saints Palmatius, a Consul, and Simplicius, a Senator and their companions, Saints Anastasia and Basilissa, virgins and martyrs, Saints John and Paul, brothers, and very many others. The same likewise is attested again and again in the *Acts* of the Blessed Virgins which were martyred at Rome,—as Saints Martina, Tatiana, Prisca, Theodora, Cantianilla and her brothers, Lucy, Flora, Susanna, and an host beside.

It is highly probable that the greater part of the Christian martyrs were generally beheaded with the sword rather than the axe. This may be gathered, not only from the several *Histories* of the Saints in manuscript, as well as from the accounts taken from these with no change of language, wherein we do nearly alway read how Christ's warriors were chastised, slain, struck, punished, and so on, with the sword, but likewise from the fact that it was held more ignominious to be slain with the sword than with the axe. Thus Spartian, in his *Life of Geta,* declares how Caracalla was angered because Papinian, the famous Jurist, whom he had ordered to be put to death, was beheaded with an axe and not a sword. We say the martyrs "were *generally* beheaded with the sword," for it cannot be denied that they were likewise sometimes put to death in this fashion with the axe. Thus we find it occasionally stated in divers writers of Ecclesiastical History how they were executed with an axe, and so won victoriously the heavenly crown of martyrdom.

FASHION WHEREIN THE CHRISTIAN MARTYRS WERE BEHEADED.

Most generally the Blessed Martyrs were decapitated kneeling on their knees with the body bending forward. Thus the *Histories* of the Saints represent it, and in especial that of St. Paul the Apostle writ under the name of Linus, of St. Menna, of St. Dionysius (St. Denis), and his companions, of St. Flavian, and divers others. In the *History* of the death of St. Paul the Apostle we read, "Binding his eyes with Plautilla's handkerchief, Paul set both knees to the ground and stretched out his neck. But the soldier lifting his arms aloft, struck him with all his strength, and cut off his head." In the *Acts* of St. Menna is to be found as follows : "When he had so said, he knelt down and stretched out his neck, and was instantly beheaded with a sword;" and in those of Saints Dionysius, Rusticus, and Eleutherius, "Forasmuch therefore as the Blessed Martyrs had, to begin with, been stripped and beaten with rods in sight of all, they were now clad again in their garments and led away to the place fixed for their beheading, and there ordered to fall on their knees . . . ;" and further on, "Kneeling and with out-stretched necks, at one and the same instant, according to the Prince's order, they were beheaded with axes;" then a little further on, "An ineffable light shone round about them all, and the dead body of St. Dionysius sprang upright, and taking in his hand the holy head from the corpse . . ." Lastly, in the account of the passion of St. Flavian, it is recorded how, "When the speech was done, the victim goes down to the appointed place, and binding his eyes with the part of the chaplet which Mutanus had bidden him keep two days before, and kneeling down as though in prayer, he ended his martyrdom and his orisons at one and the same moment."

We said, as explained above, that *most generally* the blessed martyrs were beheaded with the sword, for, of course, this might be done, and was done, in divers ways. Thus in Valerius Maximus (not to mention other authors) we find it publicly stated that persons to be beheaded were very usually tied to stakes. This writer says, "He bade them to be beaten with rods, then tied to a stake and beheaded with an axe." So we read of St. Stephen, the Pope, that he was decapitated seated in his chair, and of another Christian martyr, St. Alexander, that he met the same fate standing up. Of this last it is recorded, "When he had thus addressed the crowds that were assembled, Alexander turned to the executioner and said, 'Stay a little, brother, that I may make another prayer to God.' Then, falling on his knees, he prayed thus. . . . On

FIG. XXXII.

A. Martyr struck with a club or cudgel.
B. Sawn in two with an iron saw.

C. Hands and feet cut off.

To face p. 178

178a

hearing this voice, the holy Martyr rose up from the ground, and addressing the soldiers, cried, 'Quick, my brothers, do your duty.' . . . And when he had so said, Cælestinus drew his sword, and taking a linen cloth, bound the blessed Alexander's eyes therewith."

From these passages we gather that such as were to be beheaded with the sword were used first to be scourged with rods, and then afterward their eyes to be covered over and veiled with linen cloths or handkerchiefs.

The reader is referred to what we have already quoted from the *Histories* of the martyrdom of St. Paul, St. Florian, St. Alexander, St. Dionysius and his companions, as also what we have stated on the authority of Valerius Maximus and other Ancient writers as to how the blessed martyrs were stripped and beaten with scourges before decapitation.

.Moreover, I would have the reader know how sundry Catholics have been condemned to death by beheading by the Heretics of our own day (1591), amongst whom (see Sanders' *Anglican Schism*) were especially two shining lights of England, to wit John Fisher, Bishop of Rochester, and a member of the Most Sacred College of Cardinals, and Sir Thomas More, a knight and a while before Chancellor of that whole Kingdom.

Now of the eleventh and twelfth modes of torture as named above, wherein the Blessed Martyrs were branded with disfiguring marks, or had their heads beaten with an axe or with clubs, witness is borne in the *Histories* of Saints Bibiana and Aurea, Roman virgins and martyrs, of Saints Laurence, Eutropius, Getulius, and others.

This last form of punishment, which was especially infamous, forasmuch as a free citizen's countenance was disfigured thereby, is likewise mentioned by Suetonius in his *Life of Caius*, "Many men of honourable rank he first disfigured with marks of branding, and then condemned to the mines and to work on the roads, or to wild beasts. So again Seneca, "There are divers sorts of bonds, and divers kinds of punishments,—mangling of the limbs, branding of the brow, etc. . . ." This sort of disfigurement of the face, whereby the offenders' brows were marked with deeply incised characters that could never be obliterated, was forbid by the Emperor Constantine, but restored again under the Heretic and Iconoclast Emperor Theophilus. For there is no doubt this Prince did disfigure,—nay! let us say rather, adorn,—with such brandings the faces of the two Sainted brothers, Theophanes and Theodorus. And here let us quote, for the greater glory of God and the pious profit of the faithful, what Metaphrastes hath preserved concerning the aforesaid martyrs, Saints Theophanes and Theodorus, from their letter addressed to the Bishop of Cyzicus and the rest of the multitude of Orthodox believers, "So when we stood before the Emperor's face silent and with downcast eyes, the Prince turning to the Prefect, which stood beside him, with insolent speech and truculent aspect, spake thus in an angry and rough voice, 'Take the fellows away, and inscribe and engrave on their faces the verses composed for this purpose, and deliver them over to two Saracens, that they carry them away with them to their own country';" and further on, "For it were easier for heaven and earth to be turned upside down, than to seduce us from our religion. Then did he command our countenances to be engraved; and the fiery lashes we have received from the scourges still paining us exceedingly, we were stretched on benches, and our faces stamped with words. And they went on pricking and pricking till darkness came on, when the sun set. . . . Verily shall we be known of Christ by these signs, and these letters shall be known and read of the heavenly hosts. For the Lord Himself said, 'Whatsoever ye have done unto the least of these, ye have done unto Me.'"

CHAPTER X

Of yet other Instruments and Modes of Torture for the afflicting of Christian Martyrs,—as Amputating Women's Bosoms, Cutting out the Tongue and Lopping off Hands and Feet, Pulling out the Teeth, Flaying alive, Transfixing, and Exposing to Wild Beasts

BUT it is time now to go on to other sorts of torture, beginning with that wherein women had one or both bosoms cut off, with a view to augmenting their pain to the utmost. This cruelty is attested again and again in the *Acts* of divers female martyrs,—as for instance of St. Euphemia, of Saints Dorothy, Thecla, and Erasma, three sisters, of twelve Holy Matrons whose names are forgot, of St. Agatha and others, and lastly of St. Helconis, whose sufferings are recorded in the Greek *Menology* under May 28, in these words, "Same day, the anniversary of the Blessed Martyr Helconis. She lived under the Emperor Gordian, and came from the city Thessalia. Arrested and brought before Perennius, the Governor of Corinth, she would not endure to sacrifice to idols, but preaching Christ and none other, she was first bound by the feet to an ox yoke, and laid in molten lead and boiling pitch, escaped unhurt, and was afterward shaven and her whole body drenched in fire. Being let go again, she went into the temple of idols, and by her prayers threw down to the earth the images of Pallas, Jupiter, and Æsculapius. Nay! more, when Justinus succeeded Perennius as Proconsul, her bosoms were cut off, and being brought before the new Governor, she is cast into a furnace of blazing fire; but the flames do not so much as touch her, though they burned up and consumed many of the soldiers. Afterward she was stretched out on a brass bedstead heated red-hot; but of a sudden a company of Angels stood round her, and saved the holy martyr from all harm. Next she is exposed to wild beasts, which did her no sort of hurt, but slew several of their keepers. Finally the Governor pronounced sentence, which she most gratefully received; and so she was beheaded and took her departure to heaven."

But to proceed to other modes of torture,—those to wit wherein the martyrs' teeth were dragged out, or their tongues excised, or their hands or feet, or both, amputated, or lastly their legs broken.

OF MARTYRS WHOSE TEETH WERE PULLED OUT.

This torture is attested by the *Acts* of the Holy Saints and Virgins, Apollonia, Anastasia, and Febronia.

OF MARTYRS WHOSE TONGUE WAS CUT OUT.

Christians which were subjected to this kind of punishment are named in the *Acts* of many Martyrs of either sex,—as of

Saints Terentianus, Florentius, and Hilary, Saints Basilissa, Anastasia, and Agathoclia. The last named is thus commemorated in the *Menology* under October 1 : "Anniversary of the Blessed Martyr Agathoclia, a slavewoman. She was the servant of a certain Nicolas, a Christian, and his wife Paulina ; and seeing she was a Christian and did fear God, she was daily tormented by her mistress, who for eight years was for ever striking Agathoclia on the head with sharp stones, and used to force her to walk forth barefoot to gather sticks in winter and frost, for all these eight years striving to persuade her to adore idols. But this she utterly refused to do ; so she was scourged, her tongue cut out, and cast into prison and there starved. Finally fire was poured down her throat, and she exchanged this life for a better one." The other two, Saints Basilissa and Anastasia to wit, are found thus commemorated under April 15 : "Anniversary of Saints Basilissa and Anastasia. These were natives of Rome, the capital, ladies distinguished by birth and wealth, and disciples of the Holy Apostles, and when these latter were crowned with martyrdom, they had had the holy relics collected and removed by night. For this they were denounced to the Emperor Nero, and were accordingly thrown into prison, and presently, when they remained steadfast in their profession of Christ, were brought forth again, and hung up, then after breasts, hands, feet, and tongues had been cut away, were finally beheaded."

Fig. XXXIII.

A. Martyr whose tongue is being cut out.   C. Whose breasts are being amputated.
B. Whose teeth are being drawn.

To face p. 184

OF MARTYRS WHOSE HANDS OR FEET WERE LOPPED OFF, OR THEIR LEGS BROKEN.

These three modes of torture employed upon Christians are witnessed to in the *Acts* of St. Quirinus and thirty-seven other martyrs, of Saints Severus and Memnon, of St. Charitina, virgin and martyr, of St. Galatio and his wife, St. Hadrian and his companions, to say naught of forty Roman soldiers whose holy martyrdom is recorded in the *Martyrology* under March 9.

OF DIVERS FASHIONS WHEREIN THE BLESSED MARTYRS' TEETH WERE PULLED OUT, AND THEIR TONGUES AND BREASTS CUT AWAY.

By the operation of the divine power and goodness it sometimes came about that the martyrs, after their tongue was cut out, yet uttered speech and did discourse excellently. This is attested by sundry of the *Acts* of the Blessed Martyrs above cited and by the records of the martyrdom of St. Anastasia. As a rule the Holy Martyrs had tongues and breasts cut away, and teeth pulled out, after they had first been bound to stakes set upright in the ground. This we learn from the *Acts* of St. Febronia, virgin and martyr, cited a little above.

HOW THE BLESSED MARTYRS HAD THEIR FEET CUT OFF, AND THEIR LEGS BROKEN.

The Christian martyrs' hands and feet were amputated (as is testified in the *Acts* of St. Febronia, of St. Oceanus and his companions) in this fashion. First, the limb to be removed was placed on a block of timber or stand of wood; then the executioner would lift up his arm holding the axe, and bringing this down with a crash, would strike away and lop off the part in question.

Leg-breaking was effected as follows. An anvil was got ready, and an iron bar; then the wretched criminals, or Christians, it may be, condemned to death for their fidelity to Christ, were ordered to put their shins on the anvil, which the inhuman executioner did then smash with heavy blows of the iron crowbar. This is all described in the *History* of the martyrdom of St. Hadrian, mentioned by us above.

This punishment, as likewise that of breaking of the loins, is spoke of, among Ancient writers, by Plautus in his *Poenulus*, where he saith :—

Ex syncrasto scrurifragium fecit

("The wretch was a mere hotch-potch of mangled humanity before, and now he had his legs broken into the bargain"); by Apuleius, *Golden Ass*, "Then the noble wife, praying to avert this dreadful doom and thinking with horror of his legs being broken, hides away her gallant, who is all shuddering and deadly pale with terror."

FALSE OPINION HELD BY SOME CONCERNING THIS PUNISHMENT OF LEG-BREAKING DISCUSSED.

Some are of opinion that this penalty of leg-breaking was identical with that of breaking the legs of a criminal after he was nailed to the cross. But to speak candidly, those who

FIG. XXXIV.

A. Martyr, the skin of whose face is being flayed off.
B. Whose feet are being amputated.

C. Whose legs are being broken.
D. Whose forehead is being branded.

186a

think so are utterly and entirely mistaken; for the practice of breaking the legs of persons crucified, to the end they might die the sooner, was in use only among the Jews, and not followed by the Gentiles. The latter were wont to leave the bodies of crucified criminals hanging on the cross till they rotted away. This is implied by Plautus, who in his *Miles Gloriosus* makes a slave say :—

Noli minitari ; scio crucem futuram mihi sepulcrum

("Don't keep on threatening; I know well enough the cross will be my tomb at last"); and by Horace, *Epistles :—*

Non hominem occidi, non pasces in cruce corvos

("I have not killed a man; you shall not feed the crows with my flesh on the cross").

From this it is perfectly plain the Gentiles were not used, like the Jews, to remove from the gallows the bodies of those they had crucified, but rather to leave them there to rot.

But we must go on to discuss the remaining forms of torture,—and first those wherein sharp-pointed reeds were stuck under the finger-nails, between these and the flesh of the fingers, or the martyrs flayed alive, or impaled on a sharpened stake.

These tortures are spoke of in divers accounts of the deaths of the Saints,—notably of St. Bartholomew the Apostle, as likewise of St. Glyceria, a Roman virgin and martyr, of Saints Gregory the Armenian, Galatio, Boniface, Benjamin the Deacon, and many others.

OF MARTYRS TRANSFIXED WITH SPITS.

Moreover the Blessed Christian Martyrs were not only impaled with a sharpened stake, as just described, but were likewise transfixed sometimes with iron spits. This is stated distinctly (to say naught of the *History* of the Martyrdom of St. Quirinus) by Sozomen, in his *Ecclesiastical History*, "At Gaza the populace, under the Emperor Julian the Apostate, did virulently persecute at that time Eusebius, Nestabus, and Zeno, which were Christians. They were arrested when hiding in their houses, thrown into gaol and beaten with scourges. Presently all the folk began to gather at the theatre and cry out angrily against them, declaring they had profaned their holy images and conspired in former days to destroy and insult the religion of the Heathen. So by dint of shouting and mutually exciting one another, they were lashed up into passionate anger and a fierce desire to have their blood. Thus egging each other on, as is the way of the populace when once roused to turbulence, they rush to the prison, and haling them forth, drag them along, face down, face up, as it might happen. Presently dashing them on the ground, and belabouring them with sticks and stones and whatever weapons chance put in their hands, they cruelly did them to death. I have heard, too, that the women, coming out of the weaving sheds, stabbed them with their pointed spindles, and the cooks in the market-place snatched caldrons of boiling water from their fires and dashed the contents over them, while others pierced them with their spits. Then when they

F<small>IG.</small> XXXV.

Martyrs being flayed alive.

To face p. 188

188a

had mangled their bodies and so broken their heads that the brains poured out on the ground, they convey them to a spot outside the city where dead carrion was wont to be thrown away." But enough, and more than enough, said of impaling martyrs with sharpened stakes, transfixing them with spits, and suchlike horrors.

We must now speak,—to finish the list of tortures enumerated at the beginning of Chapter IX.,—of the ways wherein the Martyrs were flayed alive, and then concerning the Catholic sufferers of our own day, under whose finger-nails needles are stuck by their Heretic persecutors.

Martyrs, in full possession of their consciousness and all their senses, often had the skin of their whole body flayed off, or sometimes that of some part only, back, face, or head, to which lighted coals were then sometimes applied.

Now concerning the torture of Orthodox believers by Heretics by means of needles driven under the finger-nails, the author of the *Anglican Controversy* thus writes of the case of Alexander Briant : "When Briant had spent two days in the Tower, he was summoned before them by the Governor of the Fortress and Doctors Hammond and Norton, which did cross-examine him in their customary fashion, proposing an oath to him, whereby to compel him to answer to all the charges brought against him. And when he would not say by whose aid he was backed up, where he had performed the Mass, or whose confessions he had heard, they ordered needles to be stuck under his finger-nails. But so far was he from losing his firmness at this cruelty that he did repeat with a cheerful mien the Psalm, *Miserere mei, Deus* (Have mercy upon me, O God), and earnestly besought God to pardon his tormentors."

But to proceed now to yet other modes of torture, whereby, as we have said already, martyrs were thrown down headlong from lofty places. That they were so treated the *Acts* of sundry martyrs attest, for instance the *Acts* of St. Clement of Ancyra and of St. Felicitas and her sons. Tacitus, the Historian, writes how one Lucius Pithuanius, a magician, was cast down from the Tarpeian rock, while Apuleius, in the Discourse wherein he doth defend himself against the charge of sorcery, saith, "A wondrous fabrication, a cunning falsehood deserving of the gaol and the dungeon." Now the Dungeon and the Tarpeian Rock were both of them names of the spot at Rome from which criminals were hurled down. Seeing then it is plain magicians or sorcerers were thrown down from this Dungeon, we cannot doubt but Christians, which were believed to be sorcerers by the Heathen, were subjected to the same form of punishment, and so won for themselves the blessed crown of martyrdom.—But enough of this ; let us go on to yet other modes of torture.

OF MARTYRS WHICH WERE TORN IN DIVERS WAYS, OR EXPOSED TO WILD BEASTS OF DIVERS KINDS.

Witness is borne of sundry of Christ's most blessed martyrs which were afflicted in these fashions in the *Histories* of divers Saints, as for instance in those of Saints Philemon and Apollonius, St. Thyrsus and his companions, St. Mark the

FIG. XXXVI.

A. Martyr pierced through with a sharp-pointed stake.
B. Martyr whose belly has been cut open and the liver torn out, which the heathen used sometimes to eat.

To face p. 190

190a

Evangelist (*Roman Martyrology*, under April 25), and St. Onesiphorus, a disciple of the Holy Apostles, St. Martiana, virgin and martyr, and an host of Saints and Martyrs which did win their crown under the Emperor Nero.

FASHION WHEREIN MARTYRS WERE DRAGGED ABOUT AND TORN.

Sometimes Martyrs were dragged (as is gathered from their *Acts* cited above) over rough and stony places, or ground sown with brambles and thistles, tied to the necks or tails of unbroke horses by ropes looped and fastened round their ankles.

Concerning Catholics, which were pitifully dragged through cities by the Heretics of our own day, you will find many particulars in the *Theatre of Heretic Cruelties,* Sanders' *Anglican Schism,* and in the work already cited *On the Anglican Persecution.* Particularly in the first named, the *Theatre of Cruelties,* you will read how a venerable widow, sixty years of age, at the city of Embrun, was bound by the hair of her head to a log of wood, and so most cruelly dragged through the streets of that place in scorn of the Catholic religion.

OF MARTYRS CONDEMNED TO THE WILD BEASTS.

Furthermore, it was customary with the Ancients in former days to condemn criminals, or Christians if it so happened, to the wild beasts. This punishment is mentioned by Asinius Pollio, Aulus Gellius, Apuleius, Athenæus, and Josephus, as well as in divers *Acts* of the Blessed Martyrs, whereby, as likewise in Suetonius' *Life of Domitian*, we are informed how that they were so exposed, not to lions only, but sometimes also to dogs, though lions were more commonly employed. We learn this not only from the story of Androcles related by Ælian, and the *History* of the Holy Martyr, St. Ignatius, as given in Eusebius' *Ecclesiastical History* and in St. Jerome, but likewise from the common cry the Roman populace was used to raise against the Christians. For Tertullian doth again and again affirm how the Roman mob was for ever crying, "The Christians to the lions, the Christians to the lions!" "If the Tiber," he writes, "overflows the walls, if the Nile does not overflow the fields, if the sky hath stood still, or the earth trembled, if famine or pestilence hath befallen, instantly is the cry raised, 'The Christians to the lions!'" And in another place: "For fear there be none left to shout, 'The Christians to the wild beasts!'"

That Christians were often cast to these kinds of animals as well as to others to be devoured and torn in pieces is shown by their own *Histories*, as well as by Tertullian, above quoted; nor is this surprising, for we find on consulting the Roman law books, it was a punishment held proper for slaves. It was usually inflicted only on slaves and persons of the viler sort, and seeing Christ's faithful servants were held of like estimation with slaves among the Heathen, it need cause no wonder if they be found very frequently exposed to the beasts.

It was not always in one and the same fashion the Blessed Martyrs were so exposed. Sometimes were they stripped naked, and shut up in the midst of theatres or other places where they were imprisoned ; sometimes were they bound to stakes, or wrapped in nets, or clothed in the skins of beasts, and so given to the lions ; sometimes with their feet fixed in hollowed stones by means of molten lead, they were enclosed in a confined space and delivered over to be worried by dogs. Witness is borne to this in the *Acts* of the Holy Martyr, St. Benignus, in these terms, "Angered by these words, the most wicked Emperor commanded him to be shut up in prison, and a great stone with a hole through it to be brought, and his feet to be fixed therein with molten lead, and red-hot bradawls to be stuck lengthwise into his fingers under the nails, and for six days neither food nor drink to be given him ; moreover that twelve very savage dogs should be imprisoned along with him, maddened with hunger and thirst, to the end these might tear him in pieces, and the gaol to be watched by soldiers. Accordingly they fixed very sharp bradawls to his hands, and confined his feet in a stone by means of molten lead, and shut up very savage dogs with him in the prison,"—and a little further on, "Oh! wondrous goodness of God, oh! fatherly love of Jesus Christ for His own ! Lo ! an Angel gave him aid, and the dogs grew gentle, so that they touched not so much as a hair of his head or a thread of his clothing. . . ." Next let us hear Eusebius speaking of Christians exposed to wild beasts, "Maturus, therefore, Sanctus, Blandina, and Attalus, the day for fighting with the beasts having been expressly fixed for the torture of them of our faith, were led out to the wild beasts, that they might afford the Heathen a public and open

spectacle full of inhumanity and cruelty. Then Maturus and
Sanctus are again exposed to every sort of torture in the
amphitheatre ; . . . and these holy men do endure the savage
worrying of beasts, and every other form of torment. . . .
But Blandina, bound aloft to a beam of wood, is offered a
prey to the beasts that rush in. Being so seen suspended as
on a cross, and praying fervently, she did instil a great zeal
and alacrity in the minds of her fellow-sufferers ; for in their
martyred sister, thus hanging on the cross before them, they
seemed in a way to see Christ Himself, which was crucified for
us, with their bodily eyes. . . . However, when not one of
the wild beasts would so much as touch her flesh, she was
presently taken down from the beam, and thrust back again
into prison." Again lower down in the same chapter he
proceeds, writing of the martyr, St. Alexander, a physician,
"The mob of the populace now began to cry out against
Alexander. When the Governor cross-questioned him, asking him who he was, he answered, 'I am a Christian.'
Whereat the Governor was sore provoked and condemns him
to the beasts. So the next day Alexander joins the same
band for fighting the beast with Attalus,—for the Governor, to
please the people, condemns Attalus a second time to this
punishment. Accordingly these two in the amphitheatre,
etc. . . . "; and a little further on again, "Last of all, Saint
Blandina, albeit a noble and well-born matron, after heart-
ening her children to their doom and sending them forward
victorious to Christ the King, now herself running the same
race of torments, going gladly to rejoin them, and exulting

FIG. XXXVII.

A. Martyr bound by either leg to the tops of two neighbouring trees, which have been bent down and forcibly drawn together, and will presently be suddenly let go again.

B. Martyr tortured by having sharp reeds stuck under his finger and toe nails.

To face p. 194

194a

with a great joy in her own death, was hastening not as though to be cruelly cast forth to the beasts, but as one happily invited to the marriage feast of the bridegroom. So after scourging and mangling' by beasts and roasting in a frying-pan, she was finally rolled in a net and exposed to be tossed by bulls. And after she had been mangled and thrown about for a long space by these animals, but had no feeling whatever of the tortures so far applied to her, partly by reason of the hope wherewith she trusted in God's promises, partly through the discourses she held betwixt herself and Christ, she was eventually slain by a sword-cut in the throat."

To quote Eusebius once more: "Of these we know well how some won glory in Palestine by their patient endurance of torments, and others acquired great renown at Tyre in Phœnicia. And who is there has not marvelled above measure at these men, when he beheld the countless scourgings they endured, their fighting with wild beasts, and endurance of the attacks of leopards, huge bears, savage boars and bulls roused to madness by fire and steel, and the wondrous fortitude of these noble-hearted martyrs against the assault of each and every beast? At the doing of these things we were present ourselves, and noted how the divine power of our Saviour, Jesus Christ Himself, to whom they were giving noble witness in their tortures, gave a very present help at that time to His martyrs and manifestly showed itself to them.

"For those ravening beasts durst not for a long while touch the bodies of the Saints or so much as approach near them, whereas they were ready to rush upon those unbelievers, which, standing without the barriers, one here and another there, did incite and tar them on to attack the victims. And albeit the blessed soldiers of God stood there naked in the midst, and provoked them with gestures and tried to bring them to assail them (for they had been expressly commanded so to do), yet they were the only ones the creatures would not touch. Indeed, several times when they did rush out upon them, they were repelled, as though by some heavenly power or influence, and leapt back again quicker than they had come. And when this was seen to happen over and over again, it did excite no scant wonder in the heathen which saw it, so much so that when one beast made a vain attack, they would loose a second, and then a third, at one and the same martyr.

"Meantime one might well be lost in wonder and astonishment to see not alone the manly and intrepid temper of these Holy Men's minds, but likewise the firm and inflexible constancy exhibited by those of quite tender years. For you would behold a mere stripling not twenty years old yet, constrained by no bonds, yet standing firm, his arms extended each side to form a cross, with gallant and lofty determination pouring forth prayers to God, his attention never wavering, not moving a whit to one side or the other from the spot where he stood,—and this while bears and leopards were breathing rage and death against him, and actually trying to tear his flesh with their teeth. But their mouths, by some divine and mysterious power, were stopped,

I know not how, and the creatures hastily fled back again of their own accord."

One last quotation from Eusebius on this subject, who speaks repeatedly of Christ's faithful servants being exposed to wild beasts: "Others again you might see,—for there were five of them in all,—offered to the horns of a huge wild bull. This monster did toss in the air several of the unbelievers which came near, and mangled them miserably, and left them half dead to be dragged away by the hands of their companions; but to the holy martyrs, albeit it strove to rush at them, burning with rage and fury, it could not so much as come near. And albeit it sprang hither and thither with rushing feet and waving horns, and goaded on with the application of branding irons breathed terror and destruction against them, yet was it held back and forced to withdraw by some interposition of the divine will, till at last, seeing it could do them no hurt, other beasts were loosed against them instead. At long last, after many and divers attacks and assaults of these animals, the martyrs were slain with a sword and committed to the waves of the sea by way of burial."

Now that the martyrs were likewise delivered by the Heathen to be torn of dogs, clad to this end in the hides of beasts, is shown (to say naught of Christian witnesses) by Cornelius Tacitus, the Roman Historian and writer on morals, who saith in the *Annals:* "So to stifle this rumour (that he had set Rome on fire himself), he brought to trial and subjected to the most exquisite torments those whom the common folk, to express their contempt and hatred of them, called Christians. The originator of this title was one Christ, who, under the Emperor Tiberius, was punished by the Procurator Pontius Pilate. The mischievous superstition was suppressed for the time being, but presently brake out again, not only throughout Judæa, the original seat of the evil, but even in the Capital itself, to which everything abominable and disgraceful collects from every quarter, and multiplies. Accordingly such as confessed themselves Christians were first arrested, and at their denunciation a vast multitude of others; these were proved guilty not so much of having actually fired the city as of general malevolence to mankind at large. Moreover mockery was added to the death penalty in their case; clad in the skins of beasts, they were exposed to be torn to death by dogs, or were nailed to crosses, or were set up to be burned, and after daylight failed, used as torches to give light." See likewise the *Roman Martyrology* under June 24, where an almost identical account is given of these Saints' deaths, and which speaks generally of many Christians which won the crown of martyrdom under Nero.

We read, moreover, in Eusebius' *Ecclesiastical History*, as well as in the *Acts* of divers Blessed Martyrs, and especially in those of Pope Marcellus, how Bishops of the Church, under the Emperor Maxentius, were for their greater degradation assigned to look after beasts of burden. So in the *History* of Marcellus, Bishop of Rome, it is found writ, "He was imprisoned and attacked because he was for setting the

FIG. XXXVIII.

A. Martyr imprisoned in a net, and so exposed to be tossed by a savage bull.

B. Thrown down naked to be devoured by wild beasts.

C. Wrapped in a wild beast's hide, and so left to be torn by animals.

D. His feet fixed in a great stone, and with red-hot brad-awls stuck under his finger-nails, the martyr is given over to be worried by starving dogs.

To face p. 198

Church in order, and being arrested by Maxentius and required to deny that he was a Bishop and demean himself by sacrifice to demons. But consistently despising and deriding Maxentius' orders, he was condemned to the stable-yard, that is the stalls or stable of the beasts of burden, or in other words to feed (as Eusebius doth explain in another passage) the Emperor's horses and camels, which were used for the public service in carrying loads.

Read further in Theodoretus' *Ecclesiastical History* what he saith of St. Hormisdas, a Persian martyr: "There was a certain Hormisdas, of the first nobility among the Persians, sprung of the race of the Achaemenidae, and whose father had been Governor of a Province. Learning that this man was a Christian, Goraranes, son of Isdigerdis, King of the Persians, orders him to be summoned before him and to abjure God his Saviour. But Hormisdas cried, 'What you command, oh! King, is neither just nor expedient, for whoso-ever hath learned readily to despise God, which is the ruler of all men, and to deny Him, will be so much the more ready to contemn his King, since the latter is but a man and a participator in human weakness. . . . But the King of Persia, which should have admired his wise speech, did rob God's noble champion of his wealth and honours, and gave him orders to strip off all his garments except only a breech-cloth, and lead the camels that were in his army. Now when many days were past, and the King, looking down from his raised seat, saw that excellent nobleman scorched by the sun's rays and all covered with dust, calling to mind his former rank and splendour, orders him first of all to be brought to him, and a linen shift to be thrown about him. Then, supposing his mind must be softened, whether by his past hardships or the kindness now manifested towards him, he appeals to him, saying, 'Come, now, put away your obstinacy, and deny the carpenter's son.' But Hormisdas, fired with divine zeal, tore the shift in twain and, tossing it in the King's face, accosts him thus, 'An if you think I shall desert my faith for this thing's sake, take back your gift and your impious thought with it.' . . ." A punishment of the same kind is recorded by Victor, in his work *On the Vandal Persecution*, wherein, speaking of Armagastus, a most noble martyr of Christ, he saith, "Then doth Theodoric condemn him to exile in the Province of Byzacium, and there to be employed in digging of ditches. Afterward, as if to further disgrace and dishonour him, he orders him to act as a cow-tender not far from Carthage, where all men might see him."—But to proceed now to other matters.

OF CHRISTIAN MARTYRS GIVEN TO MICE TO BE NIBBLED OF THEM, OR TO HORSES TO BE TRODDEN UNDER FOOT.

Christians were given to mice by Goraranes, the most cruel of the Persian Kings, as Theodoretus relates in his *History,* "Moreover they dig pits, put them (the Christians) very carefully into them, and turn in upon them a vast number of shrew-mice. Finally, after binding their hands and feet to hinder them from driving off the little creatures, they would offer them as food to the mice, which under the stress of

FIG. XXXIX.

| A.A. Martyrs bound to the neck or tail of wild horses and cruelly dragged about. | B. Drawn through the streets or over stony places by means of ropes attached to their feet. |

To face p. 200

hunger gradually ate away the flesh of the imprisoned saints, thus torturing them horribly day after day. . . ."

More or less similar, though even more cruel, appears one wherewith the Heretics of our own time (1591),—as described in the work entitled *Theatre of Heretic Cruelties*,—do vex and torment the Catholics. Laying them on their backs and binding them so, they place on their bare belly inverted basins with live dormice shut up inside them, and light a fire over the basins, so that the dormice, excited by the heat, may gnaw their bellies and bury themselves in their inwards. This most painful and horrible torture has been applied in our own time to numbers of Catholics, to make them abjure their Faith. Of these were some moreover that were ready, like the Christians which did suffer under Nero, to be sewn up in the hides of beasts and exposed to the bites of mad dogs (at the orders of Elizabeth, Queen of England), rather than fulfil her wicked commands, and fail or fall off the slightest from the true Catholic Faith.

Likewise of Christian martyrs, and especially of Bishops, which were cast on the earth by the orders of impious persecutors, and so trampled and mangled by horses, Victor doth bear witness in his *Vandal Persecution:* "After these cruel edicts so full of noxious poison, he orders all the Bishops, which had been assembled at Carthage, and whose churches, houses and substance, wheresoever they had taken up their abode, he had begun to plunder, after being so robbed, to be driven forth of the city walls, not an animal or a slave, a single change of raiment being left them, adding to boot that anyone which should offer any of them hospitality or give them food, or should attempt to do so out of pity, would be burnt up with fire, he and his house with him. Then did the expelled Bishops act very wisely; for adopting the state of mendicants, they did not quit the city at all, knowing well that if they did withdraw, they would only be recalled again and forcibly brought back, and moreover that their enemies would lie, as they had lied before, and declare they had run away because they were afraid-to face the contest, and last but not least that, if they did so return, they would find no place of refuge open to them, their Churches, their houses and their goods being all seized.

"So as they were lying groaning round about the circuit of the walls and exposed to the weather, it fell out that the King went forth to the baths. To him they all crowded eagerly, saying, 'Why are we so afflicted? For what faults unwittingly committed do we suffer this treatment? If we were called together to hold a disputation, why have we been plundered? why are we driven out, and put off? why, deprived of our Churches and our houses, are we made to bear hunger and nakedness, and left wallowing in the mire?' But looking at them with lowering eyes, even before he had heard their appeal, he ordered horses with riders on their backs to be driven over them, that they might not merely be bruised and hurt by this violence, but actually killed. And indeed many were trodden to death, especially the older and weaker amongst their number."

Imitating these examples, the Heretics of our own day

treated in like fashion a certain friar, John by name, a venerable member of the Order of St. Francis, and lately appointed Bishop of Daventry. After wounding him most savagely and hurting and insulting him in divers other ways, they trod him under foot, and left him lying in the streets like a foul and abject corpse. We read of the same being done under the Emperor Diocletian to three Blessed Saints of Christ, Maxima, Secunda and Donatilla, virgins and martyrs.—But enough here; the remainder of the divers tortures enumerated at the beginning of Chapter IX. must be reserved for another chapter.

CHAPTER XI

Of other Tortures and Modes of Martyrdom,—Burying alive, Throwing into Rivers, Wells, or Lime-kilns, Cutting open the Belly, and the like

THE further tortures, whereby martyrs were cast into deep ditches and buried with earth, or hurled into a running stream, or into wells, or else into a lime-kiln, are attested by many *Histories* of Martyrdom, and particularly in those of Saints Castullus, Vitalis, Marcellus, Philemon and his companions, Saints Paulina and Daria, Roman virgins and martyrs, Saints Calistus and Carisius, Saints Alexandra, Claudia, and Euphrasia, matrons, Julitta, virgin and martyr, Saints Florus and Laurus, and many others. The two last named are commemorated in the *Menology* under August 17 in these words, "Anniversary of the Blessed Martyrs, Saints Florus and Laurus. These holy men were twin brethren, and hewers of stone, an art they had learned from Proclus and Maximus. But after their masters had suffered martyrdom for Christ's sake, they left Byzantium (Constantinople) and retired into the district of Illyricum, to the city of Ulpiani, where, working in the quarries under Licio the Governor, they worthily followed their trade.

Fig. XL.

A.A. Martyrs cast into deep pits and buried up to the neck with earth and stones.

B. Martyrs half buried, with arms tied behind them, and so left to perish.

To face p. 204

Finally, after enduring many tortures and being cast by Licio into a deep well, they gave up their souls to God."

Further, that the blessed martyrs were also thrown sometimes into a lime-kiln is manifested by the *Acts* of St. Clement, Bishop of Ancyra, as likewise by the account of three hundred martyrs given in the *Roman Martyrology*, under August 24 : "At Carthage, anniversary of three hundred Holy Martyrs in the time of Valerian and Gallienus. Amongst other punishments, after the Governor had commanded a lime-kiln to be lighted, and in his presence live coals and incense to be brought forward, he said to the three hundred, 'Choose ye one of two things,—either offer incense to Jupiter on these coals, or be plunged into the quicklime.' Then, armed with faith and confessing Christ the Son of God, they threw themselves with a quick dash into the fire, and amid the vapours of the quicklime were instantaneously reduced to powder. Whereby that white-clad host of Saints did well earn the title of the White Band."

HOW THE BLESSED MARTYRS WERE USED TO BE BURIED ALIVE.

It should be stated here, before our discourse doth proceed to other points, that Christians to be tortured in this fashion were not always cast bodily into deep pits to be buried entirely under earth and stones, though they were generally. For we read in the *Acts,* just cited, of Saints Philemon and Marcellus, that these martyrs for the faith were so buried only up to their loins. But the reader may, an he will, read their *History* for himself.

OF DIVERS MODES WHEREIN CHRISTIAN MARTYRS WERE CAST INTO THE SEA OR INTO RIVERS.

Not alway in one and the same, but in many divers fashions, are the Blessed Martyrs recorded to have been thrown into the waters. Sometimes this was done after great stones, or leaden weights, had been fastened to neck or feet or right hand, as was the case with Saints Sabinus, Agapius, Florian, Alexandra, Claudia, Euphrasia, matrons, Julitta, virgin, and others. At other times they were cast in with hands and feet tied, or wrapped in a net, or shut in leaden boxes, or sewn up in a bag. These modes are attested in the accounts of the martyrdom of Saints Faustinus and Jovita, as also of Saints Hermillus, Ulpian, Stratonicus, Nicostratus, and others.

We must here inform the reader that *the bag* was a very ancient form of punishment indeed. Plautus makes mention of it in his *Vidularia* in the words :—

Jube hunc insui culeo, atque in altum deportari, si vis annonam bonam

("Order the man to be sewn up in a bag, and cast into the deep, if you would have a good harvest"). Now the bag here spoke of was a skin, or sack made of leather, wherein murderers were sewn up, together with a dog, a cock, a snake, an ape, or at any rate some of these creatures, and thrown headlong, such was the Roman law, into sea or river. From very ancient times a law of the sort seems to have existed in the case of parricides ; thus Cicero saith, "If any man have

FIG. XLI.

A.A. Martyrs cast down headlong from a height. | B. Thrown into a lime-kiln.

To face p. 305

206b

killed his parents, or beaten the same, and be condemned on
that count, his head is to be wrapped in a˙ wolf's skin,
wooden shoes (that is, fetters) to be put upon his feet, and
he is to be led to prison, there to] tarry a little, while the
bag is making ready wherein he must be put and so cast into
the water."

The fact is, this law was passed by the Romans to terrify
others from copying the ensample of Lucius Hostius, who
was the first of mankind, after the War with Hannibal, to
kill his own father, and taking their parents' life with the
sword or otherwise. Accordingly, when during the Cimbrian
War (A.U.C. 640) Poblicius Malleolus murdered his mother,
he was punished in this fashion. His fate is mentioned by
Livy in these words, "Poblicius Malleolus, for the murder
of his mother, was the first ever sewn up in a bag and thrown
into the sea," and in another place, "Malleolus was condemned for his mother's murder. After sentence, his head
was immediately muffled in a wolf's skin, while the bag was
getting ready, wherein he was to be put and so thrown into
the water." At a later date Pompey the Great, when Consul,
passed a law, further amending the ancient ordinance, extend-
ing the degree of relationship within which murder involved
this form of punishment, and detailing the creatures to be
enclosed in the bag along with the culprit,—to wit, a dog,
a cock, a viper, and an ape. The same law of Pompey's is
again recited, with identical provisions, by Justinian in the
Institutes. True, this law fell into practical disuse in later
Roman times by reason of the cruelty of its provisions ; but it

was revived for the benefit of the Christians, several of whom won their crown of martyrdom in this strange fashion.

OF ORTHODOX CHRISTIANS CAST BY HERETICS INTO THE SEA AND RIVERS, OR BURIED IN THE GROUND.

Victor, Bishop of Utica, doth describe in his *Vandal Persecution* how the Catholics were embarked by their Heretic persecutors on board derelict ships, without sails or oars, and so committed to the vasty sea to confront certain shipwreck. Nor is it only the Heretics of olden days we hear of as casting away Catholics on the waters, but those of more modern times as well. This is attested in the *Theatre of Cruelties* in these words, "When the city of Oudenarde in Flanders had been occupied by the host of the Gueux, these insurgents laid hold of all the priests of that province which were noted for piety and learning and carried them off to the castle. Amongst these was one, Master Peter, a venerable old man and the oldest of all the company; after heaping divers insults and acts of violence upon him, they stripped him of his clothes, bound his hands and feet together behind his back, and threw him headlong through the castle windows into the river, the good man crying all the time as he fell with alert and undaunted spirit, 'Thy will be done, oh, Lord." . . . In like fashion were subsequently cast down the venerable John Paul and the rest of the divines, of whom Master James, the eldest of them and a weakling, unable to swim, was carried by the waters some way thence, taken out, and his life saved." Again, somewhat lower down, "Ursula,

FIG. XLII.

A. Martyr thrown into a watercourse, with a heavy stone attached to his feet.

B. Thrown into a river enclosed in a net.

C. Thrown into a neighbouring stream, with a stone tied to his arm.

D. With a leaden weight fastened round his neck.

E. Cast head-first into a well.

To face p. 208

a Nun in the Béguinage at Haarlem, after her aged father, acting magistrate in that city, and several other well-reputed and well-born Catholics with him, had been hanged, was herself led under the gallows, and asked whether she would forsake her faith and the orthodox Religion, and marry a certain soldier. And when she steadfastly refused so to do, she was at once cast into the water, and drowned;" and again, "This one fact you must note, how the Heretics of the city of Nîmes in Languedoc, after slaughtering a great multitude of Catholics with their daggers, threw them, some dead, some still half alive, into a well in the city, which was both wide and deep, and filled the same twice over to the brim."

All this in the above named book, *The Theatre of Heretic Cruelties*, wherein likewise is found the following concerning Catholics which were buried in the earth: "The Huguenots did bury alive a certain priest named Peter, of the parish of Beaulieu, leaving his head only above ground. Other clergy in like wise, at a place in Belgium not far from Ypres, did they cover over alive with earth and stones, and setting up marks a short way from their heads, did roll therefrom bowls of stone or iron at them by way of sport."

It remains next to reveal and expound sundry other sorts of torture and torment; and first to speak of martyrs which were publicly stripped and so led naked through the streets of cities, secondly of such as were shut up in dungeons strewn with broken glass or shards of pottery or even iron caltrops, so that their bare bodies might be miserably tormented by their sharp points, and of such as were tied to the branches of

two trees and so wrenched asunder. After this it will be left
only to speak (in Chapter XII.) of martyrs driven into banishment, and those condemned to hard labour of divers sorts and
to the mines.

The first and second kinds are attested by the *Acts* of the
Blessed Martyrs, Saints Alexander and Vincent, Peter and
Marcellinus, Victor and Corona, as likewise by the *Menology,*
where, under September 9, it is recorded, "Anniversary of
the Blessed Martyr Strato, who, being bound to two cedar
trees and so rent asunder in two parts for the faith of Christ,
was made one with the celestial host." Of other faithful
servants of Christ which were subjected to the same torture,
Eusebius and Nicephorus both bear witness, as well as the
History of the martyrdom of the above-named Saints Victor
and Corona.

OF CATHOLICS, AND IN PARTICULAR MONKS AND PRIESTS, WHICH HAVE HAD THEIR BELLIES RIPPED UP BY HERETICS WITHIN THIS PRESENT CENTURY.

Not alone by the Idolaters of Antiquity, and by Heretics
of olden days, have Christian martyrs been ripped up in divers
fashions (as shown just above and in previous passages), but
likewise by the Heretics of our own day. Let us quote what is
said as to this in the *Theatre of Cruelties*, and elsewhere, "The
Huguenots at the Church of St. Macarius in Vasconia did rip
up the bellies of sundry priests, and gradually drew out their
bowels by winding the same round sticks which they did turn
about and about. In the city of Mancina, having laid hold of

Fig. XLIII.

A. Martyr shut up in a leaden box and drowned in a river.
B. Sewn up in a bag, together with a cock, a viper, an ape, and a dog, and thrown into the nearest sea or stream.

To face p. 210

a priest, a man of an advanced age, they cut off his privates, and after roasting these over a fire, did cram them into his mouth; then that they might see how he would digest the same, for he was still alive, they ripped open his belly, and so finished him. In the case of another priest, they did imitate the tyranny and cruelty of the Emperor Julian, and cutting open his belly with a sword, while he was yet alive, did stuff him full of oats, and so gave him to their horses to feed upon."

Such were some of the tortures wherewith Christ's priests were tormented. Now hear others, equally horrible and cruel, to the end we omit nothing pertaining to the glory of the Catholic martyrs that died for true Religion's sake : " In the parish of Cassenville, near Engolisma, the Huguenots seized upon a certain priest, Lewis by name, a man admitted by the general voice of the inhabitants of the place to be of an excellent and exemplary life, and plunged his hands so often and so long in a vessel full of boiling oil that the flesh was stripped and fell off from the bones. Nay! not content with this cruel torment, they did pour the same boiling liquid into his mouth, and seeing him not to be dead yet, slew him by shooting at him with leaden bullets from iron barrels. Another priest, Colin by name, they took and cut off his privates; then shut him in a cask with a hole in the top, and poured on top of him such a quantity of boiling oil that he gave up the ghost under such torments. In the parish of Rivières, they laid hands on yet another priest, whose tongue they tore out, whilst he still lived, by piercing the chin, and afterwards killed him; likewise another, named John, they murdered by cutting his throat, after first burning all the skin off his feet with a red-hot iron. . . . François Raboteau, Vicar of the parish of Foucquebrun, was seized by the Huguenots, and tied to the oxen dragging a waggon, and so savagely goaded and lashed that he died at last of the pain and torment. At the time when Prince Auriac occupied Ruremond, a city of Guelderland which he had seized, his soldiers violently assaulted the Carthusian monastery there, shouting *Geld, Geld,* signifying by this cry that they wanted money. At the entrance gate were slain three lay brothers, Albert, John, and Stephen of Ruremond; thence rushing into the Church, the soldiery disturb the venerable Prior Joachim at prayers with the rest of the Brethren. Him they wounded in several places and dragged forth, while four monks were killed on the spot, while the rest were left grievously wounded. . . . In the city of Engolsheim, a certain Friar, John Auril by name, of the Order of St. Francis, an old man of eighty, had his head split open with an axe, and his body thrown into the privies. Moreover, at the hands of the same ministers of Satan, in divers places, many priests serving God had noses and ears cut off, and eyes forced out. Indeed so audacious was the insolence of one Huguenot and so monstrous his barbarity, that he made himself a necklace of priests' ears that had been cut away, and boasted thereof before his leaders as a mark of bravery and energy. . . . Moreover the Calvinist Heretics which are in the Kingdom of England do lay violent hands on Catholic priests intent on performing the divine sacrifice, and clad as they are in their sacred vestments, set

FIG. XLIV.

A. Martyr haled through the thoroughfares of a city by means of an iron collar fixed round his neck.
B. Stripped naked and rolled over sharp iron caltrops.

212a

FIG. XLIV.

A. Martyr haled through the thoroughfares of a city by means of an iron collar fixed round his neck.
B. Stripped naked and rolled over sharp iron caltrops.

212a

them on horseback in the midday and with burning torches carried in front, lead them about the streets in mockery. They bore their ears too with a red-hot iron, and exposing them, as they do with other religious men, on a stage to the public scorn, fix their heads in the pillory, as they call it, nailing their ears at the same time to the framework thereof—and this for no other reason than their sympathising and speaking well concerning the innocence of the martyrs and other Catholics which be tortured for their orthodoxy."

Such are some of the deeds done (to say naught of others described in previous chapters and others again yet remaining to be recorded) by the Heretics of the present day in England, Ireland, France and Belgium.

CHAPTER XII

Of Martyrs driven into Exile, and condemned to Hard Labour or the Mines

IT is high time now to return from these digressions and proceed to the discussion and proof of the remaining modes of punishment employed by the Ancients for the torment of the Christian Martyrs, as enumerated in Chapter IX. These be banishment and condemning to hard labour or to the mines.

The first of these, banishment to wit, is attested by divers authors, Tertullian, Cyprian, Jerome, the last named speaking of the Holy Apostle St. John, as well as by countless *Histories* of the Blessed Martyrs, and in particular of Pope Clement, of Flavia Domitilla, of Saints Bibiana, Demetria, and Severa, virgins and martyrs.

Concerning Christians condemned to hard labour, such as digging, carrying sand and stones, and the like, see the *Histories* of divers Saints, as of Pope Clement, and of St. Severa, referred to just above, as also those of Saints Papias, and Maurus, Roman soldiers.

Of Martyrs sent to the mines we have evidence enough in

Tertullian and Cyprian, cited above, as also in Eusebius, *Ecclesiastical History,* and numerous *Acts* of the Saints, for instance those of St. Silvanus, Bishop, and thirty-nine comrades in affliction, of Saints Paphnutius and Nemesianus. The last named and his companions are commemorated in the *Martyrology* under September 10 in these words, "In Africa, anniversary of the Sainted Bishops, Nemesianus, Felix, Lucius, likewise of another Felix, Victor, Dativus, and others, which, under Valerian and Gallienus, when the rage of persecution was at its height, were, on their first steadfast profession of Christ, heavily beaten with clubs, then bound in fetters and told off to dig in the mines, and so fulfilled the struggle of a glorious martyrdom." Likewise of St. Paphnutius, under September 11, "In Egypt, anniversary of St. Paphnutius, Bishop, which was one of those confessors who, under the Emperor Maximian, were condemned, after their right eyes had been put out and left legs hamstrung, to the mines. Later, under Constantine the Great, he strove earnestly against the Arians in behalf of the Catholic Faith; and at last died in peace, glorified with many crowns." So again of St. Spiridion, under December 14, "In the island of Cyprus, anniversary of St. Spiridion, Bishop, which was one of those confessors whom Maximian, after putting out their right eyes and maiming their left legs, condemned to the mines. He was renowned for his gift of prophecy and the glory of the signs vouchsafed him, and in the Council of Nicæa (Nice) he overcame the philosopher Ethnicus, which was for insulting the Christian Religion, and brought him to the True Faith."

writes : "But all the rest, as many as they had laid hands on, they (the Arian persecutors) banished to that part of Egypt called the Great Oasis. And the bodies of such as died they at first refused to surrender to their friends, but kept them secretly unburied to satisfy their capricious spite, thinking their cruelty might so remain undiscovered. Wherein these foolish folk made a great error ; for the friends and relations of the murdered men, rejoicing in their confession of the truth, yet mourning exceedingly the concealing of their dead bodies, and loudly proclaiming the cruelty of what was done, caused the tragedy of their enemies' atrocities to be more and more noised abroad. Both in Egypt and in Africa they drave many Bishops and priests into exile, . . . whom they hurried away with such violence that some died on the way, others perished in banishment, more than thirty Bishops of the Church in all being exiled." And again in another place, "Under the Emperor Constantius, who was alway ready to second the wishes of the Arians, they succeeded in effecting the banishment from Alexandria to Armenia of two priests and three deacons. Arius moreover and Asterius, the Bishops respectively of Petra in Palestine and Petra in Arabia, they not only exiled to upper Africa, but contrived that they should suffer special contumely. Lucius too, Bishop of Adrianople, who had boldly opposed them and rebuked their wickedness, they once more bound hand and head as they had done before, and bore him away so bound into exile, where he died."

So far St. Athanasius. A short extract now from Theodoretus' *History* describing the driving into exile of Catholics under the Emperor Valens, and we must leave this part of our subject : "Sentence was delivered on the holy men, the whole people sorely lamenting in front of the tribunal, by Magnus, Count of the Provincial Treasury, to this effect, that they be expelled from Alexandria, and sent away to dwell in exile at Heliopolis, a city of Phœnicia, in the which city was never an inhabitant would endure to hear the name of Christ, for they were one and all idol worshippers. Accordingly he ordered them instantly to embark on a ship, he himself standing on the shore and brandishing a drawn sword at them, thinking to strike terror into the souls of men which had again and again wounded hostile demons with the two-edged sword of the Spirit. Then he gives final command to set sail without any provisions having been loaded in the ship or anything whatever given them to relieve the inconveniences of exile."

A like barbarity doth fill the heart of Elizabeth, Queen of England, in our own day, who is now torturing her orthodox subjects with every sort of bitter torment and innumerable afflictions and penalties, sometimes (see Sanders, *Anglican Schism*) driving the same into banishment, by way of affording example and proof of her pretended clemency. But of her impiety and that of her father, Henry VIII., we have spoke elsewhere at greater length.

OF MARTYRS CONDEMNED TO HARD LABOUR, TO WIT BUILDING, OR CLEANSING SEWERS, OR WORK ON THE ROADS AND STREETS.

This sort of punishment is mentioned by Suetonius, who saith in his *Life of Nero:* "He began the artificial lake between Misenum and Avernus and the canal from Avernus to Ostia, and with a view to finishing these works, ordered all prisoners that were anywhere confined in gaol to be conveyed to Italy, and convicted persons to be condemned in every case to hard labour;" and again in *Caligula,* "Many persons of respectable condition, after first disfiguring them by branding marks, he condemned to the mines, to work on the roads, and to wild beasts." So Pliny (*Letters*), speaking of the Emperor Trajan, "Any older offenders that are discovered and such as received sentence ten years ago, let these be assigned to various tasks not much removed from penal labour; for men of this sort are commonly told off for cleansing the sewers and working on the highroads and public streets."

Further particulars concerning these punishments may be found in the *History* of Pope Marcellinus as follows : "At the time when Maximianus returned from the African province to Rome, wishing to gratify Diocletian Augustus, who was for building Thermæ (Diocletian's Baths) to be called after his own name, begins, by way of spiting the Christians, to force all soldiers of that faith, whether Romans or foreigners, to the degradation of forced labour, and in divers places to condemn the same to quarrying stone or digging sand. At the same

Fig. XLV.

| A. A. Martyrs condemned to work at the erection of public edifices. | B. C. Martyrs condemned to the labour of cutting and hewing marble blocks for building purposes. |

To face p. 220

220a

period lived a certain Christian, Thrason by name, a man of importance, and rich in this world's goods and faithful in his life ; when he saw his fellow-Christians worn out with weariness and hard labour, he would of his abundance supply food and nourishment to the holy martyrs . . . ;" and further on, "Maximian commanded that the following, Cyriacus, Largus, Smaragdus, and Sisinnius, should dig sand, and carry the same on their own shoulders to the spot where the Thermæ were being built. But amongst the rest was an old man, Saturninus by name, which was now sadly broken by age, and they began to help him in carrying his load. But when the guards saw this, how Sisinnius and Cyriacus were bearing both their own and others' burdens, . . ." The same, or very similar, accounts are given in the records of the passion of St. Cyriacus and his companions, and of St. Severa, virgin and martyr.

St. Athanasius makes mention of the same mode of punishment, "The old Bishops the Arians drove into exile, disposing of some in the stone-quarries,* and hounding others to death ;" as also Victor even more frequently in his *Vandal*

---

* Stone quarries (*lapidicinæ*), places whence stone is extracted, called in Greek *latumiæ*. Hence prisons are called *latumiæ,* either because criminals were sent there to quarry stone, or because the Tyrants of Syracuse had near that city great stone quarries excavated in the rock like a gaol, from which the stones had been hewn for building the city originally, and made use of these as prisons.

[It will be remembered how the unhappy survivors of the disastrous Athenian expedition, under Lamachus (B.C. 415), against Syracuse, perished in these *latumiæ.*]

Persecution, where he writes in one place, " But when the tyrant failed in this fashion to break down the wall of their constancy, he devises the plan of suffering none of the men of our Religion that held office in his Court to touch the usual allowances and pay, further contriving to wear them out with rustic labours. He orders well-born and delicately nurtured men to the plain of Utica to cut the field crops under the blaze of the burning sun, whither all betook themselves rejoicing in the Lord."

From all which we may conclude without a shadow of doubt that it was customary with the Ancients to tell off offenders and Christians to hard labour by way of inflicting the greatest possible injury and insult upon them, and particularly on such as were ennobled by military service. Properly speaking, it was only persons of the viler sort that were usually assigned to public works ; and if soldiers were so treated, this was directly contrary to the laws, which forbade a soldier to be condemned to the mines or to be tortured, and under no circumstances to be forced to labour at building operations or perform the daily tasks of slaves.

A building that was constructed by the sweat and toil of Christian soldiers and Christian martyrs is that enormous pile which to this day we call *The Baths of Diocletian*. This circumstance cannot but make us assign it to the special favour of Almighty God, that in later years, when Pope Pius IV. was seated on the Papal throne, the most important part of the said building, which remained intact, was changed to serve as a Church, and solemnly and duly consecrated to Mary the Mother of God and the Holy Angels (Church of Santa Maria degli Angeli at Rome). But enough concerning Christian sufferers condemned to forced labour.

OF MARTYRS CONDEMNED TO THE MINES.

Many were the sufferings and indignities we are told of as endured by persons condemned to the mines. To begin with they were disfigured with marks and brandings, and deprived of all their goods and of the Roman citizenship, if they possessed it; then they were beaten with cudgels, and loaded with fetters; compelled to lie on the bare earth, if they wanted to rest their weary limbs; tormented with filthy, stinking surroundings and by periods of fasting. Moreover the crown of the head was shaven; and lastly in the case of the holy martyrs condemned to this punishment under the Emperors Maximian, Diocletian and Galerius, the right eye was plucked out and the left leg hamstrung.

That those sent to the mines were degraded by marking and branding is plainly proven by a passage already quoted in this chapter from Suetonius' *Life of Caligula*, "Many persons of respectable condition, after first disfiguring them by branding marks, he condemned to the mines. . . ." Constantine on the other hand, writing to Eumelius in a rescript dated from Cabillunum (Châlons-sur-Saône), .March 21, Consulship for the fourth time of Constantine Augustus and Licinius :—"If any man have been condemned to penal imprisonment or to the mines in punishment of the crimes he hath been convicted of, no writing is to be made on his face, albeit on hands or ankles the sentence of his condemnation may be set in one, and one only, branding. The human face, which was formed in the likeness of the divine beauty, should never be spoiled and degraded." Thus Constantine, the first Christian Emperor, clearly showing us by his words that up to his day the practice had continued of branding the faces of such as were condemned to the mines with black marks that could never be obliterated and deep-cut letters.

As to confiscation of property and deprivation of citizenship, this may be seen from sundry laws. Furthermore, those condemned to the mines were reduced to the condition of slaves, as is again proven by a reference to Roman law, from which it followed necessarily that each article of their goods became public property on their condemnation. "A man condemned to the mine becomes a slave in virtue of his punishment, and accordingly they which have undergone this sentence have their goods confiscated to the benefit of the treasury. Wherefore any property possessed by the person whom you state to have been subsequently released by our clemency, belongs rather to the public revenue than to himself."

Further, that the Blessed Martyrs condemned to the mines were beaten with cudgels, bound with fetters, had the one half of their heads shaven, were tortured with hunger, filth and foul stenches, and the like, is manifested in one of St. Cyprian's *Letters,* addressed to Nemesianus and the other martyrs, his companions, then imprisoned in the mines: "But that you should have been so sore beaten with cudgels and tormented, by these pains making a first beginning and initiation of your confession of faith in Christ, is indeed a thing to stir one's indignation. Yet hath no Christian ever shuddered at the cudgels, seeing his hope is all in another instrument of wood, the cross. Christ's servant hath known the sacrament of his salvation ; by the cross of wood hath he been redeemed to eternal life ; by the cross advanced to the crown of blessed-ness. What wonder is it, I ask you, if, vessels of gold and silver, you have been sent to the mine, which is the true home of gold and silver, except only that now is the nature of the mines changed, and the places which were heretofore used to supply gold and silver, begin to receive the same ? They have set fetters moreover on your feet and bound your holy limbs, those temples of God, with degrading chains,—as if the spirit could be bound fast with the body, or your gold be soiled with the contact of iron. To such as are dedicated to God's service and testify His faith by their religious life, these things are weapons, not bonds ; it is not to shame they fetter the legs of Christian men, but to the glory and brightness of perfection. Oh ! feet happily fettered, that shall not be released by the smith, but by God Himself ! Oh ! feet happily fettered, which are started on the blessed road to Paradise ! Oh ! feet tied and bound now for a brief space, that they may be free for ever hereafter ! Oh ! feet that stumble for a while shackled with chains and cross-bars, but will soon run in the glorious path that leadeth to Christ ! What matter if envious and ill-conditioned cruelty hold you in its chains and bonds, when you will so soon be

Q

leaving this earth and these pains for the kingdoms of the sky? True, in the mines the body is not pampered with beds and bedding, but it is comforted with the refreshment and consolation of Christ. Your toil-wearied carcasses lie on the bare ground, but it is surely no punishment to lie with Christ. Your limbs are always squalid with scurf and foulness for lack of baths; but you are washen internally in the Spirit. Your bread is scanty and unclean; but a man doth not live by bread alone, but by the word of God. You shiver, and have naught to cover you; but he who puts on Christ is clad and warmed abundantly. Your heads are half shorn, and the hair rough and ragged; but when Christ is your head, how beautiful must that head be, which is called after the name of the Lord. All this deformity, that is hateful and abominable in the eyes of the Heathen, what splendour shall be accounted worthy of it?"

Very similar are the words of the following letter sent back by the sufferers in question to St. Cyprian: "Our fellow-prisoners give much thanks to thee, under God, most beloved Cyprian, for that thou hast refreshed their labouring breast with thy letter, hast healed their limbs bruised by the cudgels, hast loosed their feet bound in the stocks, hast made complete again the hair of their half-shaven poll, hast enlightened the gloom of the dungeon, hast levelled the mountainous places of the mine, hast even set fragrant flowers before their nostrils and shut out the choking smell of smoke. Moreover thy ministration, and that of our most beloved Quirinus, have been fulfilled, and the provisions sent to be distributed by

Herennianus the Sub-deacon and Lucanus, Maximus and Amantius, the acolytes, applied to make up whatever was lacking to our bodily sustenance."

Lastly, we know from the *Roman Martyrology* and from Eusebius that martyrs condemned to the mines often had the right eye torn out and the sinews of the left leg cut. Eusebius writes, "When presently Diocletian and Maximian were wearied with the excess of the sufferings inflicted on us and tired out with the slaughter of human beings, when they were now sated and oversated with bloodshed, and had come to feel such clemency and mercy as was to be expected of them, to avoid the appearance of exercising any special cruelty upon us for the future,—for they professed it was not seemly to contaminate States with domestic bloodshed, nor to stain with the blot of inhumanity their Empire, which all held to be so clement and full of pity, but rather that all mankind should enjoy the blessings of a genuine and merciful royal rule, and none should henceforth be punished with death, and this kind of penalty be remitted and relaxed towards us,—these benignant Princes directed merely that our eyes be torn out, and one leg broken! For in their view these were mild tortures and very gentle punishment for us to endure. Accordingly it is impossible to tell the number of those who, in deference to their horrid gentleness, have had their right eyes dug out with daggers (and the places whence they were torn seared with a hot iron), and their left legs fired at the articulation of the joints, and themselves afterward condemned to the copper mines in divers provinces, not so much to take advantage of their labour as to torture and torment them."

Further, St. Clement implies that Christians condemned to the mines were used to be guarded by soldiers; and the law dealing with the subject informs us they were regularly coerced with such stripes as are given to slaves.

Eutropius tells us Tarquinius Superbus was the first Roman to devise this punishment of the mines; but he certainly was not the first and original discoverer thereof, for Diodorus Siculus and Suidas both declare in so many words that Semiramis, the Queen of Assyria, worked mines, and did so by the help of prisoners of war. Women as well as men were sometimes condemned to labour in the mines.

OF INSULTS AND INDIGNITIES PRACTISED BOTH BY HEATHENS AND BY HERETICS UPON THE DEAD BODIES OF THE BLESSED MARTYRS.

We have already seen from St. Athanasius, in a passage quoted above regarding the exiled Catholics, how the enemies of the Christian and Orthodox Faith not alone exercised their cruelty upon the Blessed Martyrs when yet alive, but likewise upon their dead corpses. So we deem it will not be altogether foreign to our subject if we say something, before concluding, concerning the inhumanity and savagery of persecutors toward the bodies of martyrs when lacking life and feeling. To begin with, Eusebius, in the *Ecclesiastical History*, doth give many ensamples of these horrors, whereof we will quote one or two. In one place he writes: "For Cæsar, having

answered by letter, ordering that all such as confessed the
Faith of Christ should be put to the torture, the Governor,
as though to make a spectacle and fine parade of them to
the mob, commanded the Blessed Martyrs to be brought
forward into the judgment-hall. There he once more
examines them, and gives sentence that any who are Roman
citizens be beheaded, but the remainder delivered over to the
beasts." . . . Then after the said Saints had victoriously won
the crown of martyrdom, the Historian adds : " But even so
their rage and cruelty against the Saints were not satisfied,
for verily these savage, barbarous folk were stirred up by
a savage, furious beast, the Devil. Scarce, or not at all,
did they slacken their rage ; but began to exercise afresh
on the dead bodies of their victims their insults and
malevolence. For albeit these had been overborne by the
martyrs' constancy, yet forasmuch as they had put off all
human feeling, their madness was not a whit retarded or
repressed ; rather was the bitter spite both of governor and
people more and more hotly kindled. . . . Wherefore the
dead bodies of them the pestiferous stench of the prison
had choked, and torture had slain, are exposed to be mangled
by dogs, and, moreover, carefully watched day and night, that
none of our part commit them to the tomb. Finally, however,
the limbs of the martyrs slain in the amphitheatre, any that
is which had not yet been devoured by beasts or consumed
by fire, were either rent into small pieces or burned up like
coal; moreover the heads of such as had been decapitated
were collected and laid with the trunks, and for several days

guarded by pickets, to make sure of their being left unburied. . . . Meantime many folk came to mock these poor remains, and to cry, 'Where is their God now? What has their religion profited them, which they preferred to their own lives?' . . . Neither by taking advantage of night, nor by offering heavy bribes, could aught be effected by their friends ; but the bodies were alway carefully watched, the Heathen appearing to deem it a great thing gained, for them to be left lying unburied. Last of all, after the martyrs' remains had lain six whole nights and days under the open sky and subject to every ignominy, they were first burned at the hands of vile and abandoned wretches and reduced to ashes, then thrown broadcast in the Rhone, which flows near, to the end no trace of them should be left anywhere upon the earth." And again : "But the remainder of the Christian band were bound with chains, and driven by the officers on board boats, which were then launched right out into the deep sea and stormy waves. Such of these servants of the Great King as had after their death been decently and becomingly committed to the earth in burial, these the Emperors, the reputed masters, formally ordered to be dug up again and cast into the sea, lest if they were deposited in tombs and commemorated by monuments, folk should deem them gods and honour them with religious veneration." And in another place : "But this monster of cruelty (the Tribune Maxys), proceeding to yet further extremities of inhumanity, and every day increasing his almost bestial rage against men of piety, altogether transcended the laws of nature, going so

far as insolently to begrudge burial to the lifeless bodies
of the Saints; and to this end did order their corpses, left
out under the open sky for beasts to mangle, to be carefully
watched night and day. Accordingly a great number of
men might for many days be seen fulfilling this harsh and
barbarous duty, while others again kept a heedful look-out
from a watch tower or high place to see that no corpse was
fetched away. So wild beasts, dogs, and birds of prey tore
their limbs and scattered their remains hither and thither;
till the whole city was strewn everywhere with the entrails
and bones of men. At the last even such as had hitherto
been hostile to us declared they had never known aught
more atrocious and dreadful, commiserating not so much
the misfortune of the individuals so terribly treated as the
insult to their own self-respect and the claims of nature, the
common parent of all mankind. For the spectacle of human
flesh, not merely being devoured in one spot, but lying torn
and mangled everywhere (surpassing the power of pen to
describe or tragedy to represent), was offered to the eyes
of all at every gate of the city, while some even declared they
had seen separate limbs or even whole corpses, to say nothing
of fragments of human entrails, actually inside the gates.

"But now hear a great marvel! During several days
when these things were a-doing, this miracle was to be seen.
Though the weather was perfectly fine, the sun shining brightly,
the air clear, and the whole sky calm and beautiful, suddenly
the pillars throughout the city supporting the colonnades
both of public and private buildings began to exude copious

drops, as it were of tears. The Forum too and the streets, though no vestige of rain fell, grew wet in some mysterious way as though drenched with water; so that the word passed everywhere from mouth to mouth that mother earth could not longer tolerate the wickedness and impiety of the atrocities then committed, but was in some inexplicable fashion shedding floods of tears, the very stones and all inanimate nature weeping these odious crimes and justly rebuking the iron hardheartedness of men and their nature that was so cruel and so lacking in proper pitifulness."

So far Eusebius, who is further confirmed in what he saith on this head by Theodoretus and by Sozomen in their *Ecclesiastical Histories,* the former speaking of the Emperor Valens, the latter of Julian the Apostate. Theodoretus writes, "After Palladius, a man greatly given over to superstition, had done torturing the tender bodies of Catholic boys, some of these, when their martyrdom was consummated, were left lying, defrauded of due burial. So their parents, brethren, kinsmen, and I may say the whole city, claimed this one boon, this last solace, might be granted them. But oh! for the pitiless harshness of their judge, or rather their executioner!—they who fought so gallantly for their religion, they meet the same fate as murderers, and their corpses are left unburied; they who wrestled so stoutly for the Faith, they are exposed to be devoured by birds and beasts; nay! more, such as took pity on the fathers of these martyrs slain for conscience' sake, are themselves beheaded as though guilty of an odious crime."

FIG. XLVI.

Trophy composed of well-nigh all the divers sorts of instruments used for torturing the Blessed Martyrs.

To face p. 232

Lastly, Sozomen has the following passage : "But when as they had torn their bodies in pieces (to wit Saints Eusebius, Nestabus and Zeno) and so broken their heads that the brains ran out on the ground, they convey them to a place outside the city where the carcasses of dead animals were used to be thrown. Then lighting a pile, they burn their bodies ; but the bones left over, which the fire had not entirely consumed, they mix up with camels' or asses' bones that were lying thereabout,—in such wise as to make it exceeding hard to find the blessed martyrs' relics amid so many bones. Yet did they not remain for long so hid away."

Such then the tortures and torments, thus far described by me, wherewith the Christian martyrs of either sex were afflicted, and through which, in times of persecution, they won their way to the glorious crown of martyrdom.

These, oh! gallant soldiers of God, these, oh! unconquered champions of Christ, these, I say, be the bright insignia of your victory, the manifest signs of your faith and fortitude, these the marks of your triumph! Death, which ye sought so eagerly, ye glorious warriors of God's army, hath earned you an everlasting life of gladness. Ye, ye alone are truly happy! Who but shall proclaim your blessedness complete, for that holding wealth and this world's pleasures of none account for Christ's sake, ye have desired above all things else to pour out the last breath of life amid direst torments? Wherefore, in time of persecution, when the anguish of your sufferings grew more and more, fixing the eyes of your soul on the celestial guerdon, ye spake thus to God in your hearts without movement of the lips : " Here on earth, most gracious Lord God! let the torments of the body be multiplied an hundredfold, that there in Paradise gladness and peace may be increased. Oh! breasts burning with the flame of love divine, oh! hearts kindled with the ardour of the Holy Spirit!"

In no wise is it to be marvelled at, if these most gallant athletes of God, abiding in the midst of storms, were deterred by no perils, but rendered only the more eager and strenuous by suffering, did thirstily crave that every hour new and ever new tortures, the most bitter and most agonising, might be wrought on them, as though they could never have enough of pain.

But oh! wretches that we be, oh! unhappy sinners! What excuse, what excuse, I ask, shall we find before the Lord in the terrible day of His judgment, we who with no horrors of persecution to endure, no torments to affront, have held God's grace and our own salvation of so small account as to choose to pass all our life in a mere torpor of indolent sleep? What excuse shall we plead, when the very pillars of the heavens shall tremble,—when all the nations of the earth shall cry aloud,—when the most noble army of Christ's blessed martyrs, standing up before the throne of glory in great joy and confidence, shall display the scars of their wounds shining out upon their bodies and surpassing the sun's splendour with their proper brightness? What shall we then have to show? —what merits to bring forward? What plea shall we have to make?—God's grace and word inviolable? renunciation of all earthly joys, alms, fasting, and mortification of the flesh? pity, patience, and gentle compunction? peace of heart, holy, calm, and prayerful watchings? Blessed indeed they, and thrice happy, which shall possess such shields to guard them! They shall be made companions of the Holy Martyrs, and sharers and partakers in their glory!

So we do beg and beseech you, and entreat you earnestly with reiterated prayers, oh! martyrs most blessed, which for God's sake and by His holy grace, did endure torments willingly and with a cheerful countenance, and for that cause be now made one with Him in sweet accord and loving blessedness, we do entreat you to plead with God for us miserable sinners, weighed down under the most grievous offences and degraded by the most sordid sins of negligence, —that loving Him with all our heart and all our strength in this vale of tears, we may hereafter be found worthy in that dreadful day when all secrets shall be made manifest, to obtain mercy and salvation everlasting.

And above all, I do beseech you, most glorious soldiers of Almighty God, forget not me, the author of this book, which am the most abject of sinners. 'Tis by your intercession, and that only, I do hope and aspire, with all the unction and eager desire of my heart, to win everlasting felicity, and with you to be fulfilled of the abundant waters of God's bliss, and intoxicate with the unspeakable riches of the mansions of His house.

THE END.

INDEX

237

Index

Index

Index

Index

PLYMOUTH
WILLIAM BRENDON AND SON
PRINTERS

Printed in Great Britain
by Amazon

41965909R00202